Last Stone Standing

WHY WE DO IT THE WAY WE DO?

Maxwell Stuart Graham

Wigglesworth Press

Published By Wigglesworth Press
Suite 201 Punda Little, Strand Road,
Rosslare, Co. Wexford,
Ireland.

ISBN 9780 9821939-4-5

"I must recall these people who no one will ever know, whose names are not written in any historical movement, in any genealogy, in any story of the propagation of the faith, these men and women who are content simply to be true and pious and unknown Christians."
Jaques Ellul.

This book is dedicated to the unknown and dedicated followers of Jesus Christ.

Contents

INTRODUCTION

A great number of people are confused about what it means to be an authentic Christian. They are confused because the contemporary church is out of line with the original church. Things that are secondary and belong at the periphery of Christian thought and activity have been given great importance and brought to the center. In the process those elements that should have been at the center and made the priority have been minimized or lost.

Jesus is the cornerstone of the church structure. The cornerstone is the first stone laid and on which all the succeeding stones take their alignment.

When his disciples were praising the structure of the Temple in Jerusalem Jesus responded:

> *"You see all these things do you not? Truly, I say unto you, there will be not left here one stone standing upon another, that will not be thrown down"* (Matthew 24:1-2)

At the end of the day, all the stones that comprise the contemporary church structure; the positions; the buildings; the liturgy; the programs; etc. will be cast down as nothing. The only stone remaining, the last stone standing will be the great Cornerstone, Jesus Christ himself.

This book presents some of the historical, cultural and political 'stones' that became part of the building of the church. Whether it is right for them to be there is a matter of opinion. You be the judge. The purpose of this book is to give you the information you need to make an informed decision as to which of today's Christian practices are necessary for living the authentic Christian life.

So read on and find out why the contemporary church does what it does in the way that it does it.

CHAPTER ONE
History: 6,000 BC – 400 BC

It is Sunday morning and the regular church service is underway. Suddenly Demas, a time travelling first century Christian, drops in. He immediately recognizes the large building and the sanctuary with its altar table as the focal point. As he walks down the aisle he sees the podium, or pulpit, and recognizes it as the special place where the priest or pastor will stand and speak. Although the instruments are different, he is also familiar with the music group and the choir of massed singers. Looking around him he recognizes the robes, vestments and the special 'Sunday clothes' worn by the leaders and the people.

Given time to become familiar with other aspects of church life, he would recognize the top down management structure of the institution. In other words he would recognize a priest or pastor exercising authority through staff members. He would also be familiar with a culture that places a man in a superior position to a woman.

Yes, Demas would be very familiar with all these various components that we hold as being a necessary part of our regular church life.

The problem is, that although all of these things were present in his culture and in his time, they were part of the pagan world that he, as a Christian, had been called out of. He would recognize these things, but he would not connect them to his own Christian experience in the first century. Demas would probably turn tail and head for the exit while thanking Jesus that he no longer needed any of that.

We, on the other hand, do connect all these things to our Christian experience in the twenty-first century. Where we have a problem is in seeing how they connect to the church of the first century. That is why this book is subtitled, 'Why Do We Do It The Way We Do?' The 'It', of course, is 'Church'. Specifically the contemporary church and the practices that have resulted from centuries of change.

For us to understand the history of the church, the changes that have taken place and the additions to its core practices, we need to understand its beginnings.

Jesus was a Jew, and the original twelve disciples were all Jews. Christianity, or *The Way*, as it was originally called, began as a sect within mainstream Judaism.

Paul wrote to Timothy that:

'All scripture is given by inspiration of God, and is profitable for doctrine, for reproof, for correction, for instruction in righteousness: That the man of God may be perfect, thoroughly furnished unto all good works.'(2Timothy 3:16-17).

The Scripture Paul was referring to was the Jewish Tanakh, which is the collective name for the Law, the Prophets and the Writings. (Christians of today call it the Old Testament). In our search to understand the beginnings of the church it is necessary to know something of Judaism and the beginnings of the Jewish nation. We have to do so because this was the setting within which the Christian church was birthed. We need to discover the history of the Jewish nation within the context of world history.

For example, we can only really understand the United States of today if we know something of its past history. That history is entwined with the history of the world around it. The reason Columbus set sail is found in the history of Spain at that time. The reason the Pilgrim Fathers went to America and founded their colony, is to be found in the history of Europe at that time. Reasons for the events of 1776 in the USA are to be found in the history of England and Europe at that time. The reason for the USA to enter World War II is to be found in the history of what was happening in the world at that time.

Within Judea and the surrounding area, both Jew and Gentile converts to Christianity would have known the local history of their time. However, in the wider Roman Empire most of the Gentile converts knew very little of the history of the Jewish nation. Yet, to fully understand the Scriptural settings for the prophecies and promises about the Messiah, they needed to know the history of the nation of Israel. They needed to know how the events in the Scriptures related to the events in history. So just as we saw with the history of the USA, Israel's history is entwined with the history of the world surrounding it.

The Bed Rock of History and Scripture

The Scriptures begin with Genesis and the Creation. This is not the place for the Evolution versus Creation debate, but I will just touch on it before moving on. Evolution is generally accepted and taught in the secular world as being an unquestionable fact. However, there are Creation Science websites that present evidence that Evolution is an unproven theory rather than an unquestionable fact. They base this on the large number of scientific facts drawn from every area of science that do not support the theory. This is the dilemma presented to Christians of today but this was not so for the early church.

The early church did not question Creation because they took the Law, the Prophets and the Writings to be the truth from God. Jesus himself referred to them and did not deny their truth. So for the early church, the Garden of Eden where man was created was an actual place.

6,000 BC to 2,000 BC

Historians and archaeologists tell us that the earliest evidence of civilization in the world is from around 6,000 BC in what is called, the *Neolithic Age*. The evidence comes from pottery found in the area we call Mesopotamia, which means, "the land between the rivers". Those rivers are the Euphrates and the Tigris, and today we call that area *Iraq*. Archaeological evidence also shows that from that time on, mankind progressively inhabited certain areas of the earth and then began expanding into others.

By 3,000 BC, civilization began to appear in other areas of the world too. Further east in India, civilization began around the River Indus (modern Pakistan) and at the same time, the Hwang Ho civilization began in China. The early church accepted Scriptural truth, and so they saw the origin of these and other people groups as part of the table of nations in Genesis chapters ten and eleven.

The area where the first civilizations were birthed is known as the *Fertile Crescent*. (MAP p.9) The Fertile Crescent starts in Mesopotamia, curves up and round and down through Aram (modern day Syria), through Canaan (modern Israel), and ends up in Egypt. From 4,000 BC up to the time of Christ several great empires rose and fell within this Fertile Crescent.

One of them was Egypt. Contrary to what many of today's Christians believe, the children of Israel did not provide the slave labor to build the pyramids in Egypt. The Egyptians built the pyramids, including the Great Pyramid of the Pharaoh Cheops, around 2,500 BC. This was 500 years *before* Abram was born.

Abram lived around 2,000 BC at the time known as the Bronze Age. He lived in a city called Ur of the Chaldeans. Ur was a center of moon worship and was thought to be the largest city in the world at that time, having 65,000 inhabitants.[i]

It was from Ur, situated at the lower end of the Fertile Crescent, that Abram went to Haran. In Genesis chapter twelve we read that it was from there, under God's direction, that he set off for Canaan.

Putting this event into a wider context, it was while Abraham was hearing God's promises about Canaan, that the Druids in England were building their new facility, which today, we call "Stonehenge".

2,000 BC to 1,000 BC

Joseph, Abraham's great grandson, was the one who brought his descendants into Egypt around 1,900 BC. They stayed there for about 400 years until Moses led them out again. This event is known as the "Exodus" and there are various opinions as to the exact date when it happened. This makes it difficult to give a precise date for some of the earlier events in Biblical history.

For example, the Book of Judges tells of the leadership of Israel by people such as Deborah and

Gideon. Depending on which date of the Exodus you use, it was either when Deborah and Barrack fought the Canaanites (Judges Ch.4.) or when Gideon was fighting the Midianites. (Judges Ch.6&7), that in 1190 BC, the Greek kings outraged by Helen's adultery were besieging the city of Troy, and (according to Hollywood with the help of Brad Pitt), they ended the siege by sneaking into the city in a wooden horse.

Some of the dates of Biblical events can be confirmed by archaeological finds that link them to historical events in the surrounding Empires. For example: one of the earliest is a granite slab, or stele, found in the tomb of pharaoh Merneptah. This has references to Israel in the time of the Judges.

The time of the Judges was the time when the Bronze Age gave way to the Iron Age. One of the many empires in the area was that of the Hittites. Their area included much of what we call Turkey today. They were the ones who first worked with iron and brought about the end of the Bronze Age around 1200 BC.

1,000 BC to 400 BC
The time of the Judges was followed by the time of the Kings, beginning with King Saul. The young David slew Goliath and eventually became King after Saul. He ruled Israel in 1,000 BC.

To put this time into worldwide context, this was when the fierce tribes in Britain and Europe were building huge hill forts. These were huge earthen work defensive positions built on high ground. They were still in use when the Romans invaded. The largest one in Britain is Maiden Castle in the county of Dorset. It gets its name from the Celtic *mai-dun*, which means "great hill". Its remains, which eventually covered forty-seven acres, can still be seen today.

At this same time, over in Central America, the Maya civilization was just becoming established. Today, the huge pyramid structures that they built are a great tourist attraction.

Chapter twelve of the First Book of Kings tells us that after King David's son Solomon died, the nation was split into two. Ten tribes in the north became the Kingdom of Israel, and the two tribes in the south became the Kingdom of Judah. Each one was ruled by a series of kings, some of them served and obeyed God but most of them did not and so suffered the consequences.

This is when the Assyrians became dominant and set up their powerful empire. (MAP p.9) They were a very fierce and cruel people and terrorized the surrounding nations. Surprisingly though, they were also scientific. They invented latitude and longitude as well as the 360-degree measuring of a circle.

It was these same Assyrians, who in 721 BC, as written in chapter seventeen of the Second Book of Kings, defeated the ten tribes in the Northern Kingdom of Israel and took them away to captivity. The ten tribes disappeared from history from that time on. We don't know what happened to them, but about 150 years ago in Victorian England some people, who called themselves the British Israelites, floated the idea that the Anglo-Saxon people were the descendants of the ten tribes of Israel. This claim was made at the time when the British Empire was the greatest the world had ever seen dominating a quarter of the earth's population. The

British Israelites claim seems to be based more on pride than historical evidence.

Chapter twenty-five of the Second Book of Kings tells how, in 585 BC when the Babylonians came to power, they exiled the rich and educated members of the two remaining tribes living in the kingdom of Judah. (Map p.10) Archaeologists have found Babylonian clay tablets from that time which mention the daily food allotted to King Jehoiachin of Judah. (See 2 Kings 25:27)

In 539 BC the Persians overran the Babylonian Empire. It was around this time that Buddha was born in India, and Confucius was born in China. The Persian Empire (Map p.10) was the largest the world had seen up until that time. It stretched from modern day Turkey in the west, to modern day Pakistan in the east. We can read in Ezra chapter six and Nehemiah chapters six and nine what happened when the Babylonian king, Cyrus, allowed the Jewish people to return to their homeland.

This brings us up to about 400 years before Jesus was born and it is at this point that we will, for a while, leave this broad-brush view of the history of the nations and the Bible.

We've seen that it was a time of struggle for ascendancy; for control of the fertile areas and the resources and the manpower that came from subjugating a neighboring group. Above all, it was about power; power to dominate and control the physical world.

There was another world out there too. It was the world of the spiritual; of religion, of ideas and philosophy. So now we will look at these other factors that influenced the way people of the time viewed their world.

The Fertile Crescent

The Assyrian Empire

The Babylonian Empire

The Persian Empire

CHAPTER TWO

Religion And Philosophy

1: The Spiritual World

In chapter one we had a broad-brush view of the history of the nations and the Bible from Neolithic times up to 400 BC. We saw that it was a time of struggle for ascendancy; for control of the fertile areas and the resources and the manpower that came from subjugating a neighboring group. Above all, it was about power; power to dominate and control the physical world.

There was another world out there too. It was the world of the spiritual, of religion, of ideas and philosophy. Understanding something of the way the people of that time regarded spiritual matters helps us understand the world into which the church was born. More importantly it reveals the background of the pagan thought patterns that soon began to infiltrate and change the early Christian church. Some of these changes are still with us today.

As time passed and civilization developed and spread, there were moves to understand, control, or appease the spiritual forces that man discerned in the world.

For Abraham, and the Jewish nation as it developed, this problem was resolved by God's revelation of himself. As we see in the first two of the Ten Commandments, they were commanded to worship the one true and only God.

They were what we call *monotheistic,* meaning that the Jews were a 'One God' people. However, this was not so for the people of the surrounding cultures.

From the beginning, and as the centuries passed, new religions were birthed. Each one brought with it its own pantheon of gods and goddesses. Each of these gods and goddesses represented some aspect of life, for example, the Roman god Mars was the god of war, and Venus was the goddess of love.

As the old empires clashed and one of them became dominant, there was an inevitable transfer of culture and ideas. A modern day example of this process is the way that English is spoken so widely around the world today. For example, every airline pilot in the world, no matter what his nationality or where he is landing communicates with the air-traffic controller in English.

This stems from the influence the British Empire exerted on the world in the nineteenth and twentieth centuries. By 1922, the British Empire held sway over a population of about 458 million people, one quarter of the world's population at that time and covered more than 13,000,000 square miles: approximately one quarter of the Earth's total land area. [ii]

Other and obvious examples of how one culture spreads into another are the ubiquitous presence of the MacDonald's hamburger and blue jeans.

For an example of the way this happened in ancient times, we need look no further than the Egyptian goddess, Isis. Isis originated as an Egyptian goddess in 2,500 BC. She later became identified with the Greek earth mother, Demeter, who in turn was linked to the Hittite earth mother goddess Cybele and the Syrian Atargatis. Just to complicate things, Atargatis was made up of three other older Canaanite goddesses.

The worship of Isis eventually spread throughout the Greco-Roman world. Throughout the ages Isis has stuck around in one form or another, whatever the culture.

A good question to ask is whether there is any connection between Isis of the ancient cultures and the cultures in which Christianity developed and even within our culture today? The answer is, a resounding 'Yes!'

The following description of Isis, given in a book called *Metamorphoses*, written by Apuleius in Greco-Roman times, helps us see how these ancient ideas of spiritual forces are still with us today.

> *"I am nature, the Universal Mother, mistress of the elements.... sovereign of all things spiritual, Queen of the dead, Queen of the immortals, a single manifestation of all gods and goddesses that are* (she recounts the names by which she is known among different peoples), *the Egyptians who excel in ancient learning and worship me with ceremonies proper to my godhead call me by my true name, namely. Queen Isis".* [iii]

In common with many other spiritual ideas from mankind's early history, Isis, the Universal Mother, the Queen of the immortals, stayed around in man's thinking. We will see her appear again in the fourth century AD when all the pagans in the Roman Empire were proclaimed to be Christians and so brought their pagan beliefs into the church. Today we can see her in the New Age cults, nature worship, and mother-earth worship, where she is known as "Gaia".

This search for spiritual truth led mankind off in various directions, but it is not the only legacy we have from those ancient days.

We also have a legacy that comes from the search for the meaning of existence based on the intellect rather than the spirit. In other words based upon the philosophical ideas of that time.

2: The Philosophical World

Philosophy is the study of the general problems concerning existence and relies upon reasoned argument rather than on mysticism or mythology. Many aspects of Religion abounded throughout the ancient world, but Philosophy, as we know it today, was birthed in the Hellenic culture of Greece. This is a huge subject and so I only touch on it lightly.

In our day Philosophy is studied as a separate critical discipline, but back then it was not just studied, it was a way of life. This was because the principle concern was Ethics, which taught people how to live. Ethics told people what was right as well as what was wrong.

For the pagan people of that time Religion had nothing to do with deciding what was right or wrong:

> *Morality was not closely associated with religion. ..... For the most part, codes of conduct were derived from one's national customs or from the ethical teachings of the philosophical schools. ...... The wedding of ethics and religious belief, based on divine revelation, was one of the important strengths of Judaism and Christianity in the ancient world.* [iv]

Some of the issues that Paul had to address in his letters to the church in Corinth were to do with immoral behavior. Immoral, that is, in the Judeo/Christian mind-set. The pagan people of that time did not think it was immoral to have 1,000 sacred prostitutes at the temple of Aphrodite. Morality was separated from religion.

It is difficult for Christians of today to separate morality from religion. However, in our twenty-first century culture we have the Post-Modern mind-set, which is again saying that the religious absolutes of right and wrong are no longer valid. Morality is once again being divorced from Religion.

The ideas of the two ancient Greek philosophers, Socrates and Plato, have had a most long-lasting effect and still exert influence on the way people think today. On the positive side, Socrates taught that the way to solve a problem is to break it down into a series of questions, the answers to which gradually lead you to the answer. This is known as the "dialectic method" of enquiry or the "Socratic method", which we still use today.

On the negative side he also taught that virtue, all virtue, is knowledge, and that this alone is sufficient for happiness. This atheistic teaching came to the fore in the eighteenth century Age of Reason in Europe.

As for Plato, he did not have a personal god; what he proposed was an impersonal principle of perfection. He said that the reality we live in is but a shadow of the real reality and that knowing and understanding the impersonal and perfect reality is what life should be about.

He also concluded that the spiritual was inherently good and the physical was inherently evil. As we shall see in a later chapter, Neo-Platonism became a very important factor in the development of the church in its early years, particularly with regard to the Eucharist and the perceived need for it to be spiritualized.

One of the ideas that came from these pre-Christian thinkers was the ultimate reconciliation of good and evil. The Stoics of the third century BC said that no matter what happens this side of the grave, everything would eventually come into harmony. This is known as *Apocatastasis.*

The Christians who influenced the early church as it developed are known as *Church Fathers.* One of them, Origen who died in AD 254, introduced Apocatastasis into early Christian thinking when he said that eventually evil would be reconciled with God through repentance. This pagan philosophical view is at the root of the false teaching of *Universalism.*

Universalism maintains that everyone will be reconciled to God regardless of whether they have accepted, rejected or are ignorant of the atoning work of Jesus Christ at Calvary

The Biblical concept that man is body, soul and spirit was also alien to these pagan Greeks. They said that man was made up of only body and soul. There are some today who would have it that these philosophers were in some way inspired by God, but this does not hold up when what they actually said is examined against what God himself says in his word.

Over time some Jewish, Christian and later Islamic thinkers incorporated many of these philosophical viewpoints. The impact of this incorporation of pagan philosophies into Christian thinking will become evident later as we move on through the history of the church.

The world that had developed in the course of the 4,000 or so years up to the time of Jesus was fluid and ever changing. Just as the centers of political power changed and evolved, so did the philosophical and religious ideas.

With this historical overview in mind we can now take a closer look at what was happening in and around Judea, where Jesus and the church was born. We will start with the history of the 400 years that separate Malachi from Matthew, known to some as the 'silent years'.

The Greek Empire

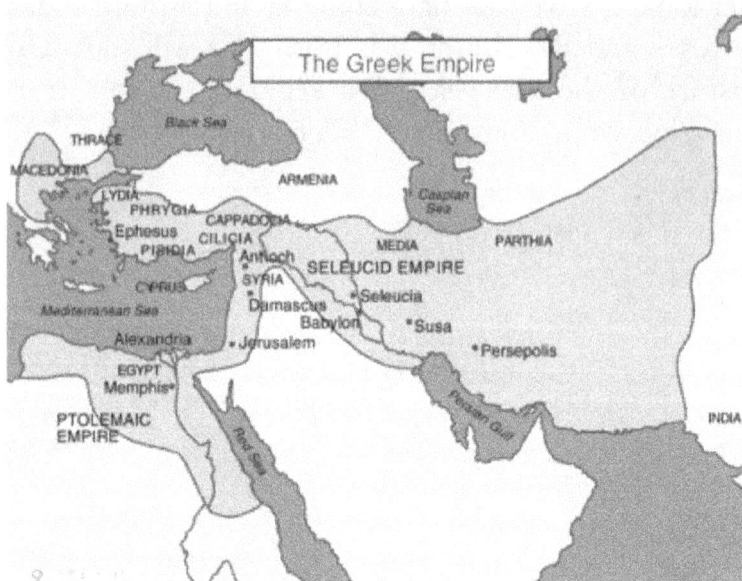

The Greek Empire

The Roman Empire

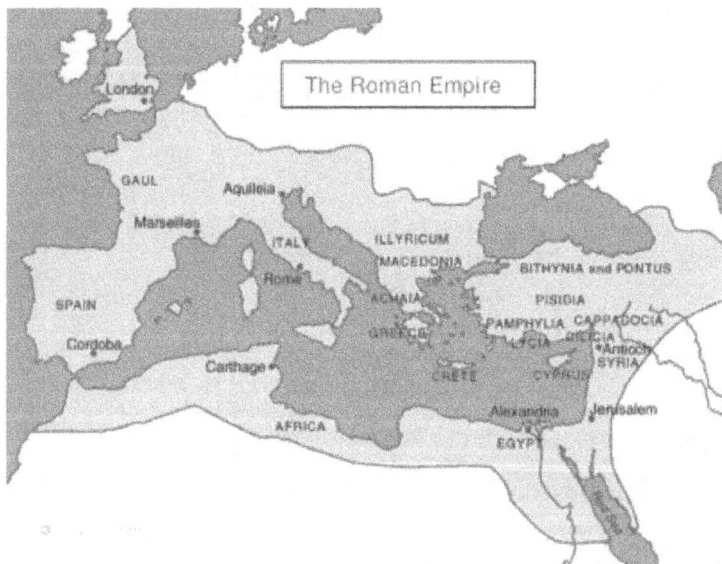

The Roman Empire

CHAPTER THREE
History: The Silent Years

The early historical, religious and philosophical developments that were addressed in the previous two chapters, bring us up to the period that began 400 years before Jesus was born.

Cyrus, the Persian ruler, had just allowed the Jewish people to return to Judea after seventy years of exile in Babylon. The Old Testament book of Malachi was written at this time. There was then a gap of 400 years between Malachi, the last book in the Old Testament, and Matthew, the first book of the New Testament.

The events of this period, generally referred to as the *Silent Years*, brought about great changes to the nation and the surrounding areas. By following these changes we can better appreciate the land and the culture of the time that Jesus, and the Christian church were birthed.

Even though the Bible is silent as to what was happening during that time we know the history of those days from other, non-Biblical sources.

The Persian Empire flourished for a time, but then as often happened in the past, another empire rose up and overran the surrounding countries. This time it was the Greeks, led by Alexander the Great. He defeated the Persians in 323 BC.

One of the reasons that he was able to make his empire the biggest that the world had ever seen up to that time, was that he recruited the armies of the conquered peoples and got them to join him.

His empire (Map p.18) stretched from the River Danube in Europe to the north; down to Egypt in Africa to the south, and from Greece in the West, to Afghanistan and Pakistan in the East.

After he died in 323 BC this huge area was split up among four of his generals creating four separate domains: Egypt, Syria, Asia Minor and Macedonia.

Alexander left a legacy that was still in place at the time the early church was born. That legacy was that the Greek, or Hellenic culture, and the Greek language, became common to all the lands of the empire, particularly those in the west.

One of the four generals who shared Alexander's empire was Ptolemy who ruled Egypt. His most famous descendant was Queen Cleopatra. She had affairs with Julius Caesar and then Mark Anthony. She committed suicide in 30 BC. She used a poisonous snake called an asp and let it bite her.

The Ptolemy's established Alexandria as one of the major cities of the ancient world. It had a lighthouse, which was one of the Seven Wonders of the World, and from around 300 BC it had a huge library of ancient books and writings. In 48 BC Julius Caesar 'accidentally' burned the library down when he set fire to his own ships.

One major edition produced for the library was the Septuagint. It is a translation of the Old Testament from Hebrew to Greek made between 300-200 BC and it is still an important source for Bible translators today.

This Greek translation was produced on the orders of King Ptolemy II of Egypt for the library in Alexandria. It was very beneficial and much needed because many of the

Jews who were dispersed throughout the empire spoke Greek and were beginning to lose their Hebrew language.

Another of the four generals who established dominions after the death of Alexander was named Seleucius. Judea eventually came under the control of his descendants, known as the Seleucids. They enforced a program of Hellenization aimed at destroying the Jewish culture.

This met with fierce resistance and it all came to a head in the reign of Antiochus IV. He issued decrees forbidding Jewish religious practices, and it is even said that he placed a pig's head in the Holy of Holies in the Temple. In 168 BC these actions led to a major revolt by the Maccabees, a group named after their leader Judas Maccabeus.

They succeeded, and in 165 BC Judas Maccabeus rededicated the Temple. The Jewish people celebrate this event up to the present day at the festival of Hanukkah, also known as the Festival of Lights. Interestingly, when Jesus declared in Jerusalem that he was 'the light of the world'. (John 8:12), it was on the last day of this festival.

For the next 100 years Judea was a free country and was ruled by a family called the Hasmoneans. They ended up in bitter family feuds and civil wars. Rome, whose empire was starting to expand eastwards, (Map p.18) was asked to get involved and take sides.

In 63 BC the Romans took over Judea, and from that time on it was the Romans who decided who ruled there.

Herod the Great came to the fore in 40 BC when the Roman senate made him the ruler of Judea. He managed this through a series of military victories, political machinations, bribery of Roman officials and murdering his rivals.

In 30 BC, the Emperor Augustus confirmed him as King. The Jews distrusted Herod because he was not a Jew; he was an Idumaean; a descendant of the Edomites who were descended from Esau. Even though he married a Hasmonean princess he was still considered to be a usurper.

He was a brutal and evil ruler who murdered his wife's family and even his own children. Beginning in 37 BC, in an effort to win favor with the Jews, he began to rebuild and expand the Temple. The on-going work was still incomplete when the Romans destroyed the Temple in AD 70.

Herod died in 4 BC, so the question is; how could he still be King when the magi who had followed the star to Jesus' birth at Bethlehem visited him? (Matt. 2:1).

The answer is because a fourth century monk, named Exiguus, got the dates wrong when he worked out the years BC (Before Christ) and AD (Anno Domini - after Christ). Jesus was actually born sometime between 8 BC and 4 BC.

There we have it, the world into which Jesus was born. It was a world formed by many empires, religions and cultures that had mixed and merged over the years; a world bounded and dominated by the legalistic and militaristic might of Rome; a world where the unifying language was Greek and the dominant culture was Hellenic.

It was a world where a Roman appointee ruled Judea but the people could still worship the one true God in their Temple, and where a multitude of gods were worshipped, but where the Emperor Augustus was hailed as the supreme deity.

> *"The contributions of Augustus of significance for early Christianity include peace, economic prosperity, improved communications, stable government, and a sense of renewal. The literature of the Augustan age celebrates the birth of a new age. There was a sense of new beginning, an old era of upheaval and warfare ended and a new era of peace and prosperity beginning. Christian authors later concurred in the sentiment, but saw in it an even deeper meaning, for Jesus had been born under Augustus' reign."[v]*

This is where Jesus was born, lived, taught, died, rose from the dead and ascended into heaven. Everything he said and did was within the context of the Jewish culture of that time and in the world of that time. His universal and eternal message is best understood in the light of that setting.

> *How much more complex is it to account for a character born 2,000 years ago into a different world, whose legacy is interpreted by so many strong-minded and independent followers? .... A reclamation project seems hopeless. Yet we do have a logical starting point. The place to begin searching for Jesus is in the world in which he grew. His roots were first-century Judaism. What was the world like for the first-century Jew?[vi]*

This we will see in the following chapter.

CHAPTER FOUR

The Land Of Judea

After the Jews returned from exile, a split developed between the two major religious groups, the Sadducees and the Pharisees. The Pharisees became centered on the synagogue, while the Sadducees were centered on the Temple.

The first Temple was the one built by King Solomon in 960 BC. The Babylonians subsequently destroyed it in 586 BC.

The second Temple was the one built in 516 BC, after the Jews had returned from their exile in Babylon.

In 37 BC, Herod the Great began a major work of refurbishing and extending this Temple. It was still unfinished in AD 70 when the Romans destroyed it. This marked the end of what is known as the *Second Temple* period.

The Temple

The Temple extension and refurbishment was an on-going major undertaking, and it employed thousands of workers of all kinds; from laborers to priests. Jerusalem was like a 'company town' in many respects. The city's economy was based on its one industry – the Temple. Its wealth was derived from the jobs created by all the building work being done, and also the income from the thousands of Jews who came there from all over the empire, especially on the Feast days.

The priests, who served in the Temple's daily rituals, were divided into twenty-four groups called *Courses*. For example, in the first chapter of Luke it says that John the

Baptist's father, Zacharias, was a priest in the course of Abia.

These priests were not part of the Temple establishment. Most of them lived outside of Jerusalem. At least twice a year members of each priestly course would leave their hometown or village and go to Jerusalem to serve in the temple.

The Temple establishment was made up of a small group of ruling families. We get an insight into this from the third chapter of Luke, which says that the High Priest, Annas, was the father-in-law of the High Priest, Caiaphas. This group and their supporters were constantly striving to protect and maintain their wealth and influence. This is an important fact to remember when reading the accounts of Jesus' trial, and when looking at the early development of the church.

The Synagogue

The Temple was one focus of Jewish life and the Synagogue was another. The synagogue system was developed during the exile in Babylon, when the Jews were separated from the Temple.

The synagogue was the center of social and religious life. It was a place of worship: a school, a social center, and a courtroom. There was no set standard model that all had to follow. Local conditions determined how it operated. There was no requirement for a Rabbi in every synagogue; but respect and authority was given to the elders, older, and more experienced members.

The Temple and the Synagogue were focal points in Jewish life, but within Judaism itself, there were many different strands and groups separated by their individual doctrines and beliefs.

Split by Faction and Party

As in most countries, the USA today has many Religious groupings: Roman Catholics and Protestants, liberal and fundamental Christians, Atheists, Muslims, Mormons, and various others. Also there are political groupings: Democrats and Republicans, Liberals and Conservatives, etc.

It was the same in Judea at the time of Jesus.

The world into which Jesus was born, for all its problems, was bursting with religious creativity. First-century Judaism was filled with debate and diversity. [vii]

In the twenty-fourth chapter of Acts there is an account of Paul's trial in front of the Procurator, Felix. Paul's accuser refers to Paul as a "ringleader of the sect of the Nazarenes." He does so because, for the first seventy years of its life, the 'Christian church' was just one of the many sects that made up mainstream Judaism.

The major religious sects at the time were the Sadducees, the Pharisees and the Essenes. Outside of 'pure' Judaism there were the Samaritans as well as the politically motivated groups such as the Herodias and the Zealots.

The Sadducees

The Sadducees were closely associated with the ruling families and fulfilled various roles, including that of maintaining the Temple. These ruling families, particularly the families from which the High Priests were selected, were descended from a group called the Hasmoneans.

The Sadducees worked hand-in-glove with the Roman rulers because it was the Romans who appointed the High Priests. In return, the Romans allowed them to maintain their positions of power.

The Sadducees did not believe in the resurrection of the dead, (Acts 23:8), nor in punishments or rewards in the afterlife. They also insisted on strict literal interpretation of the five books of Moses, the Written Torah or The Law. After the destruction of the Temple in AD 70 they disappeared as a meaningful group in the life of Judaism.

The ruling council in Judea was the Sanhedrin, and even though it was made up of both Sadducees and Pharisees, it was under the control of the Sadducees. The Sanhedrin that met and condemned Jesus was mainly made up of Sadducees. The Pharisees were out-of-towners, and they would have been at home celebrating the Passover.

The Pharisees

Modern Rabbinical Judaism traces its roots back to the group known as Pharisees. The Pharisees were centered on the synagogue and believed in the Oral Law, which was the way that the Written Law was interpreted.

The Written Law was given to Moses at Sinai, and the Pharisees believed he was also given the knowledge of how these laws should be interpreted and applied. This is something like the way the written statements in the Constitution of the United States are interpreted by the

Supreme Court for day-to-day living. It was called the "Oral Tradition" because it was not written down.

It was first written down around AD 200 in a comprehensive form known as the Mishnah, which is part of the Talmud. The Talmud is the central text of mainstream Judaism in the modern world.

The Pharisees also maintained that an after life existed, and that in the world to come God punished the wicked and rewarded the righteous. They also believed in a Messiah who would herald in an era of world peace.

Jesus' teachings often reflected, but were a higher extension of the teachings of the main schools of the Pharisees. These schools followed the teachings of two famous Rabbis, Shamai and Hillel.

"Jesus is inextricably linked to his people and their faith. To understand Jesus, we must learn to love his people and his religion. He came not to destroy but to fulfill. Hillel could have made the same statement, especially in the context of a proper interpretation of the Ten Commandments[viii]

Pharisees were in one sense, blue-collar Jews who stuck to the way of life that developed after their return from exile. They believed in individual prayer and assembly in the synagogues.

They tend to have a bad reputation because of the way that Jesus condemned them in chapter twenty-three of Matthew's gospel. However, it must be said that they too condemned hypocrites within their own ranks, just as Jesus did in.

The Essenes

They absolutely rejected the Jerusalem priesthood, who they said were descended from the illegitimate line of the Hasmoneans. They had their own High Priest who they maintained was descended from the legitimate Levitical line.

They believed in living a communal life, voluntary poverty, and the rejection of all worldly pleasures, including sex.

In 1946 many of their documents were discovered at a place called Qumran. We know them as the Dead Sea Scrolls. We can see from the writings in some of these Dead Sea Scrolls that the Essenes bitterly opposed the high priests of the Temple at that time.

The Samaritans

The Jews said that the Samaritans were the descendants of the foreign people imported into Israel to take over the land after the Assyrians exiled the ten tribes.

On the other hand the Samaritans claimed to be the "true Israel", and that Mount Gerizim was the only place to truly worship God. (See the Samaritan woman's comment to Jesus in John 4: 20).

Jews and Samaritans existed in mutual hatred and dislike. This made the message in Jesus' parable of the Good Samaritan all the more powerful to his Jewish listeners. That a hated and despised Samaritan could act in a more Godly way than a Jewish priest really pushed the point home about 'who is my neighbor'.

The Herodians

They were a political rather than religious group. Their main aim was to maintain the power and authority of the Herodian Dynasty of rulers. As such, they were on the same side as the Sadducees and, like them; they placed voluntary submission to Roman rule high on their agenda.

They were not opposed to, and even embraced, the cultural changes brought in by Hellenization and Roman ways in general. They also sided with the Pharisees in their general opposition to Jesus.

The Zealots

According to Luke 6:15, Simon, one of Jesus' disciples, was a Zealot. The Zealot's beliefs were much the same as the Pharisees, but they could not accept any foreign rule or domination. They incited the people to get rid of the occupiers by force and played a leading role in the great revolt of AD 66-70.

The Romans who at first were led by Vespasian crushed this revolt. Upon Nero's death Vespasian was suddenly proclaimed Emperor by the army in the east. Consequently he departed for Rome and left his son, Titus, to finally crush the revolt. Which he did with savage brutality.

***

So there we have it, Judea in the Second Temple period. The Temple, Synagogue, Sadducees, Pharisees, Essenes, Zealots and so on, a really mixed bag. Then along came the Nazarenes - the followers of The Way, or to give them the name that they eventually became known by - the "Christians".

CHAPTER FIVE
Emmanuel: God With Us

This book is written from the Christian perspective that acknowledges the deity of Jesus Christ. Therefore, it makes sense to take a closer look at the spiritual foundations of the church before moving on to its future physical development.

For Christians, the event of the birth of Jesus Christ marks a watershed in the development of the human race. We who live in the twenty-first century, with two thousand years of Christian tradition behind us, can often lose sight of how unique an event that was.

Christians believe that God existed before creation, and that He created all things. They believe that He is not part of the creation. He is the one who brought space and time into being.

He exists outside of the material universe and so is not limited by it. The theological term for this is "transcendence".

Paradoxically, He exists in, and extends into, all parts of the material universe He created. The theological term for this is, "immanence".

The Bible also tells us that God is Spirit. This does not mean he is a vacuum without substance. He has substance because He exists. His substance existed before, and is different from the material universe He created.

He is also Creator, Word, and Holy Spirit – the Trinity – Three in one and one in three.

Jesus revered the Scriptures and often referred to them. The early church followed His example. They believed that God formed man from the dust (the physical creation) and then breathed His life (the pre-existent Spiritual substance i.e. Himself) into man (Genesis 2:7).

God and man enjoyed a vital dynamic relationship until it was ruined by "the Fall". Restoration of that dynamic and personal relationship could only be accomplished by the actions of a perfect man/kinsman Redeemer (Genesis 3:15).

They believed that, beginning with Abraham, God began a process of developing a people through whom he would bring the Redeemer and reveal himself to the rest of mankind.

With Moses came the Law. The Law demanded a standard of behavior that was impossible to keep. Without a sacrifice to make up the shortfall it was impossible to please God.

The Law showed the people their need for a Redeemer. With its rituals of blood sacrifice and atonement, the Law presented a shadow of the reality that was to come at Calvary.

After Moses came Judges, Kings, Priests and Prophets. God used them to reveal to the people something of His own nature while at the same time exposing the true state of mankind. This was all in preparation for what was to come.

Looking back from our twenty-first century point of view, we could mistakenly assume that the people of Old Testament times had some sort of general revelation of God on a personal level. This was not so. In the 2,000-year period from when God first spoke to Abram up to the time of Jesus, God's direct contact with mankind was controlled. He limited His direct revelation and contact to a few special people who were in special situations and only for a special reason.

God revealed Himself and worked his will through people such as Moses, Gideon, Samuel, David, and Elijah. Just a handful of people - prophets, judges, priests, and kings - within a 2,000-year period.

The remainder of the 'chosen people' had no direct contact with their Creator. For the rest of humanity it was even worse. They had no knowledge of the existence of the one true God. So for all intents and purposes, humanity outside of the Jewish nation lived in a Godless void.

This was so up to around 400 BC. Then things got worse when God extended this void to include his own chosen people, Israel. From then on his chosen people, neither corporately nor individually, had any direct contact with God.

There was 400 years of silence with no prophets, no special people with the anointing and no special interventions from God into the personal or national life of the people.

The priests dealt with the function and day-to-day operation of the temple. The Scribes were the 'wise men' of the day. They were scholars with a comprehensive knowledge of the sacred writings, and they replaced the priests as the interpreters of the Law. Eventually the Scribal interpretation became the sole authority.

Except for the handful of special people alluded to above, mankind had always been totally separated from God. A small insignificant nation had been given a ritualistic formula to follow which was a shadow of the reality that was to come, but that was all.

Looking back from the beginning of the first century, we would see that for the past 400 years up to the time of the conception of John the Baptist, nobody on earth had a relationship with, inspiration from, or a true knowledge of God. This was a world apparently devoid of a real and living relationship with the Holy God.

Then came the conception of Jesus, the Kinsman Redeemer, long promised by God. As at the beginning, when God breathed His life into Adam, the Word once more formed life from created matter. This time it was with Mary, and Jesus the Kinsman Redeemer was born. This is what John was referring to when he said in his gospel:

> *In the beginning was the Word, and the Word was with God and the Word was God. The same was in the beginning with God. All things were made by him and without him was not anything made that was made.......... And the Word was made flesh, and dwelt among us, (and we beheld his glory, the glory as of the only begotten of the Father,) full of grace and truth. (John 1:1-2 and 14).*

It is only when we attempt to grasp how radical and totally shattering an event the incarnation of God was; the Word; the divine Logos coming into the world, that we can begin to understand the effect it had on people, and how they tried to deal with it.

Up to that point there was nothing in all of history or human thought that could be referred to in order to explain this event. Even the prophets of old, who had had some intimation of it from God, could not fully explain it. The disciples who lived and walked with Jesus for three years did not understand it until later. Comprehension had to wait until Pentecost, when the Holy Spirit came to teach and guide into all truth.

Jesus, the Word made flesh, came and dwelt among us. He knew what lay ahead for him. Particularly so after the Transfiguration when Moses and Elijah spoke to him about the way he was going to suffer and why. (Luke 9:31)

He taught how we could receive the gift of a restored relationship with a Holy God. He taught that this gift was going to be offered to all humanity. He taught how we should live once we had accepted this gift. He taught that we should carry this Good News to others. He taught that the Holy Spirit would come and help us in all this.

He came. He lived. He demonstrated and taught God's message of love for us. He suffered and died. He rose again, defeating Satan, sin and death. He accomplished the divine exchange and brought the fullness of salvation to all who would accept him.

He ascended to the right hand of the Father. He sent the Comforter, the Holy Spirit. He is Emmanuel - God with us, and He will come again in glory to judge the living and the dead.

The second chapter of Acts tells us how, at the feast of Pentecost, the Holy Spirit again came and combined with created flesh. The ekklesia, the called out ones, who form the universal Body of Christ, the 'church', was born. In Jesus' own words in the third chapter of John's gospel, they were "born again of the Spirit".

Jesus says that we can't enter or even see the kingdom of God unless the Spirit fills us. Our earthly flesh, i.e. created matter, has to be transformed by the Spirit (the pre-existent Spiritual substance i.e. God Himself) in order for us to have a vital connection with God. This is only possible through Jesus Christ.

"I am the Way, the Truth and the Life: no man cometh to the Father except by me". (John 14:6)

This was a totally, radical, new experience. It was human life being lived as it had never been lived before. It was God being personally experienced, as he had never been before. It was gifts of the Spirit being manifested, as they had never been before.

It was against this totally new and never before experienced life-style, that the inspiration and revelation of God was poured out and given to the people. The ekklesia, the church, was born.

The focus of the early church was Jesus, the Messiah; the Christ. The trials and the blessings of their life as born-again, regenerated human beings were secondary to their relationship with the living God and each other. They were experiencing life.

I am he that liveth, and was dead, behold I am alive for evermore. (Revelation 1:8)

In him was life and the life was the light of men. (John 1:4)

Why seek ye the living among the dead. (Luke 24:5)

The religions of the day had buildings, priests, liturgy, good works, vestments, ceremonies, etc. etc. The Christian ekklesia had no sacred places, people or things. What they did have was the indwelling presence of the living Lord, Jesus. All that 'religion' offered was dead, but what they had was "life".

For that reason Christianity was the first religion to exist without a temple, without priests, without sacrifices or an altar.

They understood that in the incarnation of Jesus (the creative Word), the link between Creator and created was restored. They understood that by his death and resurrection, Jesus overcame the forces that led to that separation and opened the way for mankind to receive the presence of God by the Holy Spirit.

They understood that the only sacred thing in the whole of creation was the Holy Spirit who indwells every born-again believer. He is present only through the faith of that believer. No external means can affect that relationship between God and man.

That is why Jesus de-sacralized everything. Nothing was sacred anymore; no more temples, no more sacrifice, no more ritual. Jesus was both the once and forever sacrifice and priest. He opened up the way into the Holy of Holies, and God would never be separated from man again.

The early Christians understood that they were the temple of the Holy Spirit; a royal priesthood, a holy nation, the temple of the Holy Spirit and set apart for God. (1 Peter.2)

They lived together in close community and were joined one to another by their common faith in the presence and leadership of Jesus. They understood that God, the Creator of all things, who had been totally separate and unknowable, was now accessible by the Holy Spirit's presence within them. They understood that the Holy Spirit was only received by faith in Jesus.

It is frequently taught that in the New Testament, God laid out a precise plan for how his church should be constructed and organized. This can only be justified by imposing twenty-first century practices on the first century texts.

What we do see when we read those texts in the context of their time, is people developing a way and a methodology for living this new life within their own particular culture and local circumstances.

The cultural, ethical, religious, and day-to-day practicalities of life in the twenty-nine churches mentioned in the New Testament, such as Ephesus, Corinth, Jerusalem, Rome, Thessalonica, etc. varied widely.

As the newly born again converts came together in each of these various places they brought with them all the cultural baggage that had been the very fabric of their lives up to that point. At the same time they were being filled with the Holy Spirit and moving into this never before experienced relationship with God.

The cornerstone of the church is Jesus Christ and these newly born again, Holy Spirit filled believers began to align their day-to-day lives with him:

"Now ye are no more strangers and foreigners, but fellow citizens with the saints, and of the household of God; and are built upon the foundations of the apostles and prophets, Jesus Christ himself being the chief cornerstone; in whom the whole building fitly framed together grows unto an holy temple in the Lord: In whom ye are also built together for an habitation of God through the Spirit."(Eph.2:19 - 22)

In the following chapters we will explore how this worked out in practical terms and the resulting changes that took place.

Unfortunately these changes moved the church away from the original pattern.   They added man-made, worldly stones, which were misaligned to Jesus Christ the Cornerstone. The building designed by the Father began to take on a different shape.

CHAPTER SIX
The Early Days

1: Phase One. The Initial Group

During the first century the newly birthed Christian church, the ekklesia, began to expand outward from Judea. In the first chapter of Acts we can see that there were around 120 people in the original Christian group.

Jesus had given them an instruction to go to the uttermost parts of the earth. After receiving the gift of the Holy Spirit, his followers were supposed to 'go', starting in Jerusalem, and eventually to the whole world. The fact is that they didn't - well not immediately.

In Acts chapter ten we read that in AD 41 Peter went to a 'God fearer', Cornelius, but not to pagan Gentiles. Around the same time, according to chapter eleven of Acts, some men of Cyprus and Cyrene did preach to some Gentiles. This is the only information we have regarding the initial outreach to the wider world.

The most obvious element that differentiated this new religion from that practiced in the Jewish synagogues and pagan temples around it was that these early Christians had no sacred building, no sacred people, nor any sacred objects.

Jesus had clearly taught that the temple age was over, that his followers would worship him in Spirit and in truth. He taught that they were temples of the indwelling Holy Spirit, and that they were a royal priesthood and a holy nation.

The Body of Christ was made up of equal and co-dependent members who recognized Christ as their only head. There was only one *"shepherd and bishop of their souls"*, Jesus Christ.

There is a great deal of information about the governance of the church during its initial start-up phase. This form of governance differed greatly from that of the hierarchical organization that developed later.

Many people think that the only early church model is the one Paul instituted in the Greco-Roman world, evidence of which we can glean from his letters and epistles. However, there was a model that predated him.

The ekklesia that formed as a result of the ministry and teachings of Jesus, and which expanded so dramatically after Pentecost, was one based in the Jewish culture.

In summary, we can observe a vibrant Messianic Jewish community flourishing in Judea before Paul ever began his ministry in the Greco-Roman world. Both the Pauline and Judean communities placed a premium on charismatic "giftings." This was evidenced through inspired preaching and supernatural healings. [ix]

Many examples can be found in the New Testament of how each member of the ekklesia was Holy Spirit led, and how the Holy Spirit's authority was recognized as paramount.

It is in the pre-Pauline ekklesia, based in Jerusalem, that we find our first examples of decision-making in the early church. These examples are drawn from the book of Acts and tell us a great deal about the activities of the first ekklesia

Remember, this was a radical and new thing in the whole of human history. An insight into how they lived it out both individually and corporately can be gained when we look at how they made these decisions.

Autonomy or Under Authority?

Having autonomy means having personal independence and the capacity to make decisions and act on them. On the other hand, being under authority takes away this independence of action.

Example #1: The decision to choose a replacement for Judas Iscariot. This is found in the first chapter of Acts, starting at verse fifteen, where we see 120 people gathered together. Peter explains to them how Judas died, and then goes on to say that they must find a replacement.

The group all pray and then they vote. They appoint Joseph and Matthias. It is notable that there was no single leader who made the decision for them.

Example #2: The decision to appoint seven people to wait on tables. This is found in the sixth chapter of Acts where it says that there was a problem because the widows were being neglected. So the twelve called on the group to find seven men who would pick up some of the workload.

The group picked seven, and the apostles prayed and laid hands on them. Again there was no single leader who made the decision for them.

Practical example #3: Stephen's decisions. The story of Stephen's decision-making starts in the sixth chapter of Acts where it says how Stephen, filled with the Holy Spirit's power, did miracles and overcame the arguments of those who disputed with him. As a result he was hauled before the Sanhedrin and tried as a blasphemer. When questioned he responded to them by giving a Bible lesson. Stephen continued challenging them until, as told in Acts chapter seven, they stoned him to death.

There is no indication that the rest of the ekklesia thought that he had made a bad decision. There is no indication that he should have remained waiting at tables. There is no indication that it was felt he should have consulted a leader.

In fact he is celebrated as the first martyr. He was an individual who made his own decision without deferring to others. No single leader made the decisions for him – nor did he ever seek approval from any 'authority' figure.

Practical example #4: Philip's decisions. Reading chapter eight in the book of Acts, we can see that Philip, just like Stephen, was another 'waiter on tables'. He decided to go to Samaria without getting approval from the apostles. It is apparent that the apostles (plural) didn't know of his decision beforehand.

When signs and wonders took place as a result of Philip's presence, the ekklesia at Jerusalem responded by sending Peter and John to find out what was going on. Philip went without 'permission' or reference to others, and the Lord blessed what he did.

When deciding who should go to see what was happening in Samaria, the ekklesia at Jerusalem acted as a group and a single leader did not make their decision.

There are other examples of this autonomous style of decision-making, which can be found in chapters nine and ten of Acts. There it says how Ananias heard from the Holy Spirit and decided to go and speak to Saul, who at that time was persecuting Christians.

Chapter ten tells how Peter had a vision and decided to visit Cornelius who was a Gentile.

It seems clear from Scripture, that at this early stage in the development of the relational groups of believers, (the ekklesia, the church), as described in the Book of Acts, there is no indication of any one person exercising authority over others.

What we do see is that there is a communal involvement in the making of communal decisions, but when making an individual decision, following the lead of the Holy Spirit was more important than getting permission from other believers.

However, within a few short years we can see that for the orderly running of the groups it was necessary to appoint 'elders', 'bishops', and 'deacons'.

2: Phase Two: Spreading The Good News

Jesus had taught for three years. He taught in Galilee and Judea but also spent time in Jerusalem, especially at the time of the great feasts such as the Passover.

Jewish pilgrims from all over the Empire came to Jerusalem for these feasts. It was to such a crowd that the disciples spoke to on the day of Pentecost, (Acts 2).

This is how the 120 people who were filled with the Holy Spirit at Pentecost became networked with a much larger and disparate group of people living in every area of the empire. In a period of forty days over 500 people saw the resurrected Jesus (1Corinthians 15:6).

In AD 35, Saul of Tarsus was on his way to Damascus to persecute the followers of Jesus. Suddenly he had a blinding vision and was knocked off his horse. Jesus told him that he was to go and preach the Gospel to the Gentiles (Acts 26:17). However, it was about another ten years before he, now known as Paul, eventually carried out the Lord's command and went.

His first missionary journey was in AD 46/47, and Barnabas, a leading member of the ekklesia at Antioch, accompanied him. At first they spoke and taught in the synagogues because the Jews would understand the prophecies concerning the Messiah. However, they were rejected by many of the Jews, and when those in Antioch in Pisidia rejected them (Acts 13), they decided to take the message to the Gentiles.

Their decision was questioned because at that time Christianity was still a sect within mainstream Judaism. However, in AD 50, at a meeting in Jerusalem chaired by James, it was agreed that the Gentiles were part of God's redemptive plan.

As time passed, an ever-increasing number of ekklesia groups were established around the Roman Empire. The New Testament refers to at least twenty-nine of them, and as time passed it became necessary to appoint *'elders'*, *'bishops'*, and *'deacons'*.

It can be argued that, at that time, all three of these terms were interchangeable because they referred to aspects of the same practical help necessary for the gatherings of the ekklesia to function smoothly.

> *The Pastoral Epistles, which are from a later period in Paul's life, seem to reveal a more formal structure of church life. The term, 'presbuteros' (elder) is used for the first time by Paul, and qualifications are given for those who would serve as 'episkopoi' (bishops) or 'diakonoi' (deacons). Adolph Harnack suggests, however, that 'presbuteros' or elder may simply denote old, as opposed to young. John Knox insists, "We are not dealing with formal offices, but with functions for which persons were certainly spiritually endowed as for prophecy and healing."(7). Kung agrees, and says that the appointing of elders "must not be seen as the beginning of a clerical ruling system." He points out that the emergence of elders/bishops must be understood in the context "of the fundamentally charismatic structure of the church (8)."* ˣ

Most importantly these people were not appointed to 'offices'. That was to come later, but at this stage in the development of the church, these people were ordinary brothers and sisters within each local group, who were seen to have the Holy Spirit gifting necessary to carry out the task.

In that sense, the Holy Spirit had already appointed them, and man was just confirming what He had done.

When reading New Testament accounts of life in the early church it is important to realize that the early church was modeled on the egalitarian synagogue model, and that the hierarchical authoritarian model, similar to that of the Temple only came later.

The rules for setting up and starting a synagogue required that there had to be a minimum of ten men. For His church, Jesus reduced this number to two or three Spirit filled believers. In a passage dealing with authority within his groups of followers he said:

"Verily I say unto you, whatsoever ye bind on earthy shall; be bound in heaven: and whatsoever ye loose on earth shall be loosed in heaven. Again I say unto you, that if two of you shall agree on earth as touching anything that they shall ask, it shall be done for them of my father which is in heaven, for where two or three are gathered together in my name, there I am in the midst of them". Matthew 18: 18 – 20.

Within the context of what Jesus was saying it is clear that he was talking about governance of the church. The church, the ekklesia, the Body of Christ, only exists where at least a minimum of two or three spiritually regenerated people come together.

{N.B. This passage is a good example of how Scripture can be misunderstood because of ignorance of the context, the culture of the day and period in which it was written.

A commonly held view today, is that this passage is referring to binding the devil. Students at the Bible College I attended were tasked to research this passage in detail and report their findings. Without exception all the students confirmed that this passage referred to church authority. Nevertheless about half of them still insisted it also referred to "binding the devil".

This misuse of Scripture is a good example of how we often override the truth of what Scripture actually says because of our own preformed opinions and prejudices.}

At this early stage in the development of the church, it still remained true to the original design with only Jesus Christ as the cornerstone.

However, as the church grew and developed throughout the Roman Empire, it was challenged by different ideas and doctrines. These challenges began to exert an influence on the life and practice of the Christian ekklesia and forced changes to the format of the egalitarian Holy Spirit led operation.

It helps our understanding of these changes in church practice, changes that we still live with today, if we know something of what was happening in the world around it. This is especially so with regard to Western Europe because Christianity, which was birthed in Judea on the eastern fringe of the Roman Empire, became rooted in Eastern and Western Europe before it spread to the rest of the world.

The Roman Empire

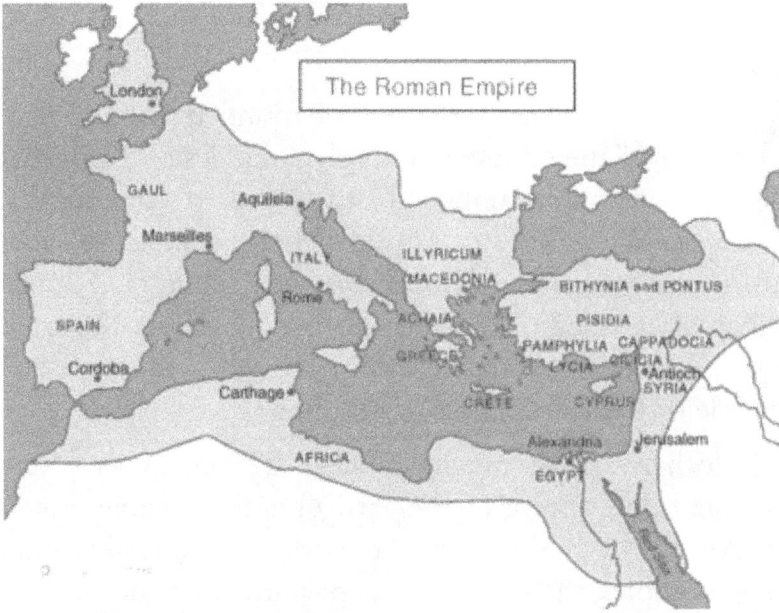

The Roman Empire

The Great Migrations

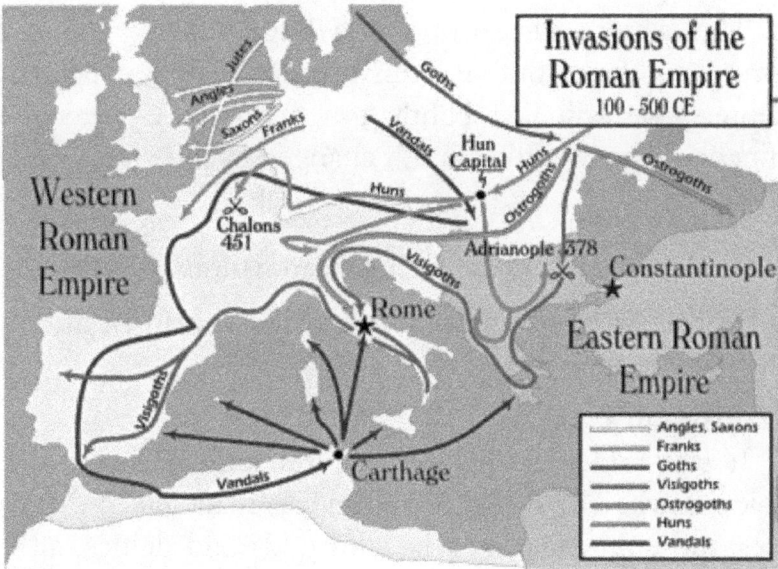

Invasions of the Roman Empire
100 - 500 CE

CHAPTER SEVEN
The Roman Empire

Introduction

At Pentecost, the Holy Spirit founded the original model of the Christian church or ekklesia. From that time on it was supposed to develop organically. Development means to unfold what is already there. Unfortunately, history shows that the church did not develop along the lines of the original model but departed from it. To depart from something means to abandon one principle or basis, in favour of another.

In other words, much of what we see in the New Testament description of the early church was abandoned and replaced by things from the world and culture around it. The complex causes of that departure from the original model are many and varied and tied into the early history of Europe.

The history of Europe is a huge subject and well worth studying, but in this and the following two chapters, we will just lightly touch on three areas that influenced the way the church changed its practices:

1. The Roman Empire

2. The development of European nations.

3. The expansion of Islam and the spread of ancient knowledge

The Roman Empire

It was said that the early church turned their world upside down. The Roman Empire was made up of diverse races and cultures with a host of gods and deities, all of whom were readily absorbed, without problems, into the wider religious, social and political systems of the day.

Even the monotheistic God of Judaism was tolerated as just another god.

However, the radical message of the gospel of Jesus Christ, as lived and preached by the early Christians brought the full force of the state to bear against them. Every effort was made to stamp out this growing faith. Rights and privileges were removed, and the most horrendous and terrible tortures and punishments were used against these Christians.

Why was this? Simply, that the gospel of Jesus Christ was the antithesis of the way the Roman world worked. The gospel attacked the very foundations upon which the orderly world of the Roman Empire was built. That foundation was an authoritarian system, which imposed itself through a rigid and hierarchical structure. Order was maintained in a uniform way throughout the Empire, taxes were collected and laws were dispensed. Each level within that structure came under the authority of the one above, and imposed its own on the one below.

In opposition to this, the gospel of Jesus Christ taught that there was only one way to God (Jesus Christ), only one leader (the Holy Spirit), and that all were equal. Christianity said that those who were to be recognized as the greatest were the servants. This was the message that turned the world upside down. This was a message that spoke of equality, freedom, and service to others.

This was the message that empowered the Christian church to overcome persecution. Tertullian said that the blood of the martyrs became the seed of the church. However, from that time until the present day, that gospel message of equality, freedom and serving others has become blurred, and in some cases, entirely lost in the Christian church at large.

Rome had been a Republic since 509 BC but this changed when Caesar Augustus was proclaimed Emperor in 27 BC. This post-republican phase is when the 'Roman Empire' began. (Map p.48)

In 65 BC Pompey the Great, a Roman statesman and general, took sides in a civil war within Judea. The end result was that Judea came under the supervision of the Roman Governor of Syria. Pontius Pilate who authorized the crucifixion of Jesus was responsible to the Governor of Syria for the smooth running of Judea.

This expansion of Rome's influence and authority reached its peak during the reign of the Emperor Trajan (died AD 117). The Empire held its own until the death of the emperor Marcus Aurelius in AD 180. From that time on it began to decline.

The Romans were practical in their exercise of power, and made the orderly running of the empire a priority.

The emperor Augustus was quoted as saying that he was surprised "that Alexander (the Great) did not regard the right ordering of the empire he had won a greater task than winning it". [xi]

They fostered the cultural legacy of Alexander's Hellenic empire and welcomed the philosophical world of Socrates, Aristotle and Plato. The Roman culture was further enriched because they absorbed the cultures of the nations they conquered and occupied.

Even as the Empire expanded its boundaries, the peace and stability established by the Emperor Augustus, was maintained. This era of stability continued under the succeeding emperors Tiberius, Caligula, Claudius and Nero.

This era of peace and stability provided just the right conditions within which the early Christian church could start to expand throughout the Empire. However, by the time that Nero died in AD 68, the Empire was beginning to experience some internal difficulties. There were many revolts, and the stable and protective Roman governmental system showed signs of breaking down.

Robbery and corruption abounded everywhere. The ruling families in Jerusalem complained to Rome but nothing was done and so finally they revolted. A Roman legion, around 5,000 men, under the command of the governor of Syria, was sent to restore order, but the Jews defeated them.

The Jews, thinking that this was the time of the promised Messiah, began a full-scale revolt against the Romans.

In AD 66 the Roman general Vespasian was sent to Judea to put down the rebellion. He arrived with two legions, eight cavalry squadrons and ten auxiliary cohorts. He marched through the land and crushed all signs of rebellion. Finally he laid siege to Jerusalem itself.

However, by this time his attention was focused elsewhere. When Nero died in AD 68 there were various contenders who wanted to succeed him as emperor. This brought about civil war and eventually one of them, Vittelius, was declared emperor.

That was not the end of it, because in AD 69, while Vespasian was in Caesarea, the armies in the east declared him to be the emperor. Leaving his son, Titus, to complete the siege of Jerusalem, he left Judea and eventually overthrew Vittelius. Vespasian was declared Emperor at Rome in AD 69.

Back in Judea, and according to early church tradition, the Holy Spirit had warned the Christians of impending disaster. They all left the city and went to Pella, a town about 60 miles N.E. of Jerusalem. The Jews in Judea viewed anyone fleeing the fight as being an unpatriotic traitor. This is seen as one of the events that led to Christianity, which up until that time had been a sect within Judaism, becoming separated from it.

In 70 AD, the Romans captured Jerusalem, and according to the historian Josephus, slaughtered, exiled and enslaved tens of thousands of Jews.

Fifty years later, a second revolt led by Bar Kokhbar, lasted from AD 132 –136 and resulted in the final defeat and dispersion of the Jewish people. Half a million Jews were slaughtered and Jerusalem was leveled. From that time on the center of Judaism moved to Galilee and beyond, to Babylon and Alexandria. The centers of Christianity had already moved away from Jerusalem.

For all its might and power the Roman Empire was still vulnerable to attack. A foretaste of what the future held for the Empire can be seen in an event that happened much earlier in AD 9. Three legions commanded by Varus marched north through the Teutoburg forest in Germania. Their guide was Arminius, a 'friendly' Germanic chieftain.

He led them into a trap and the whole three legions were annihilated. A few prisoners were taken, including Varus' young nephew. Their defeat shook the whole empire, and how it happened remained an unsolved mystery, until forty years later when the legions again moved north and rescued the surviving prisoners.

These northern Germanic tribes are just one example of the 'barbarians' who were a constant threat from outside the borders of the empire. Maintaining the peace within, while resisting those without was a constant theme, whoever was emperor.

Marcus Aurelius, emperor from AD 161-180, was a great philosopher of the Stoic tradition. In fact, he was known as the "philosopher king", a reference from Plato's works. Although much admired by historians Marcus Aurelius was also a persecutor of Christians.

He died in Vindobona (Vienna), while conducting a campaign against the Germanic tribes. He handed over the empire to his ineffectual and unstable son, Commodus, and this event is seen as the start of the great decline of the Roman Empire.

Moving forward to the year AD 305 we find the empire split in two, with a Caesar of the east, Galerius, and a Caesar of the west, Constantius. When Constantius died in Eboracum (York in northern England) in AD 306, his son Constantine the Great was declared Emperor by the army.

Ancient British history has it that Constantius' first wife, Helena, the mother of Constantine, was the daughter of the British King, Coel. According to the old English nursery rhyme this same King 'Cole' was a merry old soul and a merry old soul was he.

Roman Catholic history has Helena down as being born in Asia Minor. Seemingly, this was preferable to her being born the daughter of a "merry old" pagan king.

Constantine is often said to be the first Christian emperor, but his conversion in AD 312 is highly suspect.

In reality he remained a pagan at heart worshipping the sun, and building a statue to Cybele, the mother-goddess.

Until he died in AD 337 he kept the title Pontifex Maximus, which meant, within the pagan culture, Chief Priest. Strangely enough, in the fifteenth century, the Pope adopted this as one of his titles.

With the Edict of Milan, Constantine made the toleration of Christianity official policy. Later, he moved the hub of the Empire from Rome in the west, to the east and the city of Byzantium, renaming it "Constantinople". This eastern Roman Empire, known in modern times as the Byzantine Empire, lasted for a thousand years.

Not so the Roman Empire in the west, which only lasted until AD 476. This is when dissatisfied mercenaries, led by Odoacer, revolted, and deposed the last western emperor, Romulus Augustus. This event is generally considered to be the end of the Western Roman Empire.

Today, we can still see the evidence of this great empire in the west. For example, England has roads crossing the country, such as the Fosse Way, Ermine Street and Watling Street. These are still in use today and follow the routes surveyed and established by the Roman surveyors.

Other evidence of the widespread impact of the empire in the west is seen in the many ruins of extensive villas. They have ornate mosaics and under-floor central heating, a luxury that did not reappear for many centuries.

The pressures that led to the eventual collapse of the Roman Empire, and with it the collapse of culture, learning and language, were mainly from the host of barbarian tribes in the north and east. This decline in culture and learning led to a period known as the Dark Ages.

The Dark Ages lasted until the fourteenth century when the Renaissance began. The Renaissance was the resurgence of learning that took place throughout Europe. This event influenced the onset of the Protestant Reformation.

The barbarian invasions that led to the collapse of the Roman Empire were part of a wider event known as the Great Migration Period (Map p.48), the name given to the constant movement of large people groups across Europe.

As we will see in the following chapter it was from these people groups that the modern European nations were formed.

CHAPTER EIGHT
Europe Until AD 1500

The Development of Nations

In previous chapters we have seen how the development and history of the Jewish nation was related to the history of the nations around it. In the same way the development and history of the Christian church is related to the history of the nations of Western Europe, in which it grew and flourished.

Those nations did not appear overnight; they were the result of many years of movement and change. The Great Migration Period is the name given by historians to the years of human migration that occurred in Europe between the years AD 300-700.

The migrating peoples included the Goths, Vandals, Bulgars, Alans, Suebi, Frisians, Franks, Angles, Saxons, Jutes and the Slavic tribes. Migrations by Vikings, Hungarians, Moors, Turkic, and Mongols continued beyond the year 1000.

With our modern and neatly defined national borders, governments, international treaties and laws, it is hard for us to imagine the confusion brought about by this great flux of people groups.

For example, the Vandals were an eastern Germanic tribe who first moved west, and then went south through what is modern day France and Spain. They ended up in Tunisia in North Africa and from there they raided the underbelly of the dying Roman Empire. Eventually the

Vandals were absorbed into other people groups and faded from history in the sixth century.

In an effort to ward off the increasing attacks from these various barbarian tribes, the empire withdrew its troops from Britain in AD 407. Despite this defensive move Rome was sacked by the Visigoths (western Goths) in AD 410. The Visigoths were just one of the many Germanic tribes to invade Roman territory.

As we saw in the previous chapter, the Roman Empire in the West finally ceased to exist in AD 476, when the barbarian Odoacer deposed the last emperor, Romulus Augustus, and did not replace him.

It was out of these chaotic events that the modern European states and people groups were formed. From the start they held some things in common. Many Roman customs and traditions survived and were generally accepted. Christianity was the established religion, even though the older folk religions still flourished in some areas. Throughout Europe the common language of the ruling classes and the educated, was Latin.

The Irish were in the far west of Europe. They were a people descended from a much earlier Celtic migration. On the island of Britain, the Scots to the north were primarily the product of the original inhabitants - the Picts and the Celtic Scoti people. The Welsh are descended from the Britons who were pushed westward into Wales and Cornwall by the migrating groups of Angles, Jutes and Saxons who moved across from northern Europe.

The modern nation of England developed from these invading groups who eventually formed the Anglo-Saxon people. In turn the Danes and Vikings pressured them, and the Normans eventually conquered all of them in

1066. The Normans were a Viking people who had been settled for many years in Normandy, France. The English race is a product of these main streams of invasion.

The country of France traces its beginnings after the Franks set up a kingdom in Gaul. At first Gaul was under Roman rule, but as the Roman Empire collapsed they became autonomous. The Frankish Carolingian dynasty expanded the state and it became known as the Carolingian Empire. The country of France in the West, and the Holy Roman Empire in the East trace their origins to the Carolingians.

At one time, the Holy Roman Empire encompassed modern Germany, the Netherlands, Austria and northern Italy. It was only dissolved in 1806 during the Napoleonic wars. The modern state of Germany can also trace its roots back to the Carolingian Empire.

Modern day Spain and Portugal occupy the Iberian peninsular. In AD 415, and responding to a call from Rome, the Visigoths drove the Vandals out of the Iberian peninsular and established their own kingdom. Subsequently they succumbed to Moorish invaders from North Africa and the Iberian Peninsular became part of Islam.

Spain did not become fully Christian again until 1492 when the last Muslim enclave was destroyed. Much of the culture and architecture in Spain today reflects the legacy of this Islamic period.

In time, these various people groups settled into their new lands and became the official residents. Powerful leaders established a ruling aristocratic class. Intermarriage between them developed into dynasties, some of which still survive today. Kingdoms large and small became in turn allies, enemies and then allies again. (Map p.63)

The one unifying factor was religion - the Christian religion - because everyone in Europe from the highest to the lowest was a Christian. They all came under the authority of the ever more powerful Bishop of Rome, the Pope, who was the head of the Roman Catholic Church.

The establishment of Christianity as the accepted state religion had begun with the so-called conversion of the Emperor Constantine.

"After his victory at Milvan Bridge, faithful to his promise, Constantine favors the church from which he has received support. Catholic Christianity becomes the state religion and an exchange takes place: the church is invested with political power, and it invests the emperor with religious power, ... It is great acquiescence to the temptation Jesus himself resisted, for when Satan offers to give him all the kingdoms of the earth, Jesus refuses, but the church accepts, not realizing from whom it is receiving the kingdoms." [xii]

The rulers depended on the church to support their position of power, and the church took advantage of this by involving itself in politics.

If anyone opposed the Pope, be they king or vassal, he would be threatened with excommunication. Excommunication meant that the person could not receive the sacraments, could not attend any church service and would go straight to hell when they died. This was seen as an awesome and dreaded punishment, and the Pope used the threat of it to good effect. In this way succeeding Popes were able to exert political influence over kings and other leaders.

During this period, all the learning and the culture of centuries that had been so prevalent within the Roman Empire, was lost. Theology was confined to the monasteries where edification and worship were the goals rather than the pursuit of knowledge.

For the most part, the pursuit of knowledge was dormant and the light of 'civilization' was dimmed. Hence the name for this period is the Dark Ages.

It was a time of religious superstition and fear. On New Year's Eve in the year 1000, a great crowd gathered in Rome to await the Second Coming of Christ and the end of the world. When nothing happened, the Pope blessed them and they all went home. In the year 2000 there was similar hysteria in some parts of Christendom. You may remember Y2K, when many Christians stocked their homes with canned goods and bought guns to defend themselves in the chaos that they thought was to come. Some things don't change.

Eventually there was a stirring in the heart of Europe and the dormant period of the Dark Ages began to give way to a desire for change.

"The eleventh century was a time of new movements. There was a revival of monasticism, a new 'reform papacy' set about purging the church of corruption and there was a revival of learning. The theologian found himself faced with the question of the relation between faith (theology) and reason (philosophy)."[xiii]

The disturbance and turmoil of the Great Migration Period faded into the past, and the new nations struggled and plotted to increase their land and power.

Standing armies were unknown. Each king or ruler relied upon the loyalty of his Barons, Dukes and Earls who, in turn, would raise troops from the people who owed them loyalty.

The English King John knew he could not reign without the support of his Barons. They wanted to protect their privileges and so in 1215 in return for their support they forced him to sign the Magna Carta.

The Magna Carta is a foundational document in the development of common law in western civilization. It is the foundation of common law and of today's constitutional law, and it influenced the framing of the Constitution of the United States.

These foundations of modern society were being laid in a culture that was mostly ignorant of the ideas and philosophies of the ancient world. However, ancient knowledge and learning had not disappeared altogether.

The pre-Christian pagan philosophical ideas of Aristotle, Plato and others that would eventually influence Christian theology and practice were kept, revered and developed by another group of people. These were the people posed the next, and most alarming threat to the developing Christian world of Western Europe. These people are the Muslims, the adherents of "Islam".

Europe: Early Middle Ages

The Islamic Empire

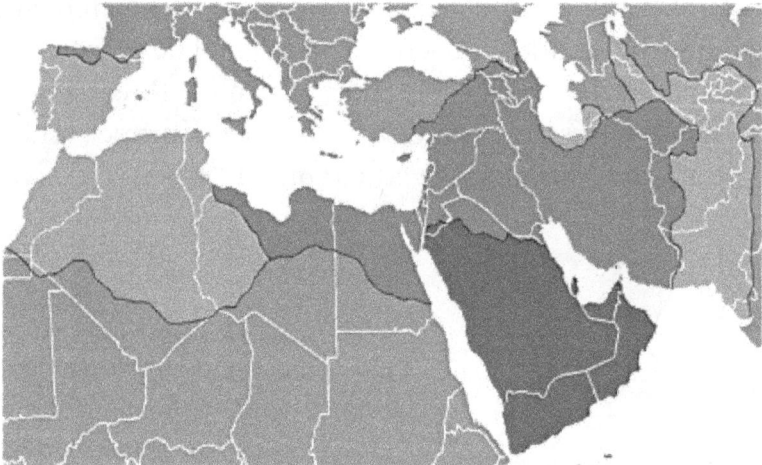

Expansion under the Prophet Muhammad, 622–632

Expansion during the Rashidun Caliphate, 632–661

Expansion during the Umayyad Caliphate, 661–750

CHAPTER NINE
Islam And The Spread Of Knowledge

1: The Expansion of Islam:

The previous chapters dealt with the end of the Roman Empire and the development of the European nations. In it we saw that the foundations of modern society were being laid in a culture that was mostly ignorant of the ideas and philosophies of the ancient world.

However, ancient knowledge and learning had not disappeared altogether. It was kept, revered and developed by another group of people. They were the ones who helped western scholars in the rediscovery of these ancient ideas and philosophies leading up to the period known as the *Renaissance*.

These people who preserved the ancient ideas and learning were the same ones who posed a threat to Christendom. They were collectively known as *Muslims*, the adherents of *Islam*.

Mohammed began preaching Islam in Mecca in the year AD 613, and then moved on to Medina. When he died in AD 632, he had united the tribes inhabiting the Arabian peninsular; the area we know today as modern Saudi Arabia.

From then until AD 631, in a period known as the *Patriarchal Caliphate*, Islam expanded rapidly and occupied much of North Africa as far west as Tripoli. To the east, the area that is modern day Iran, came under Islam. Moving northwards, it encroached upon the Byzantine Empire as far as the Turkish border.

Further expansion continued, and by the year AD 750, under the *Umayyad Caliphate,* Islam held sway over the Iberian peninsular, the Visigoth Hispania (modern day Spain) in the west, and in the east as far as Afghanistan and Pakistan. (Map p.63)

If the northward expansion of Islam into Europe had not halted, the history of Europe and of Christianity would have been very different to what it is. The expansion northward ended 150 miles south of Paris at the battle of Tours in AD 732. Charles Martel (the Hammer), a Frankish ruler and grandfather of the Emperor Charlemagne, led an army of 30,000 against a Muslim force of 80,000.[xiv]

Unlike other leaders of that time, Charles had developed a well-trained and battle-hardened army who trusted in him implicitly. Mostly infantry, heavily armed and dressed to withstand the cold, they formed up in a solid phalanx at the top of a slope.

Charles had chosen his ground well. The Muslim forces, which relied heavily on cavalry armed with spear and sword, would have to charge uphill. Heavily wooded areas prevented any flanking maneuver.

The Muslim army were not dressed for the cold weather of the north, and after several days of waiting for Charles to move out with his army, the Muslim commander, Abdul Rahman Al Ghafiqi, ordered his men in. The Frankish infantry stood firm and this became one of the rare instances in early military history where infantry were able to repulse repeated cavalry charges.

The Muslim forces suffered a great slaughter and Abdul Rahman himself was killed. The Muslim forces retreated south, back into Spain, and stayed there.

The Frankish victory was decisive and is seen by many historians as a critical point in the development of Western Europe. If Charles had been defeated there was little to have prevented the expansion of Islam into the whole of Europe.

In the east, Islamic expansion brought about prolonged outbreaks of hostilities with the Byzantine Empire. It is interesting to note that the Crusades, which were expeditions to free the Holy Land from Islamic occupation, were not a Christian idea.

"But the idea of a holy war is a direct product of the Muslim jihad. If the latter is a holy war, then obviously the fight against Muslims to defend or save Christianity has also to be a holy war. The idea of a holy war is not of Christian origin. Emperors never advanced the idea prior to the appearance of Islam".[xv]

The siege of Vienna in 1529 brought a final halt to the expansion of Islam in Eastern Europe. The Christian forces, led by the King of Poland, defeated the forces of Islam and, for the time being, the intended Islamization of Europe was suspended. In modern times this expansion of Islam into the west has taken on a more subtle approach. Instead of invading warlike armies there is a more peaceful flow of immigration into the west.

Within Islam itself there were wars, especially in the early years, and there were breakaway factions. Most of the world today is aware of the Sunnis and Shias but there are also other groups, such as the Sufis.

By the ninth century, even though Islam was no longer a monolithic Arab state, it was still held together in unity by the common ground of the Islamic faith.

Within this huge empire, with its culture of fierce warlike expansion, there was another aspect seemingly at odds to it. This was the development of ideas, of learning, science, mathematics and the cultural heritage of ancient civilizations. Hellenism, which seemed to be dead and forgotten in Europe, was one of the sources of the ancient knowledge that was preserved and developed by the Islamic scholars.

2: The Spread of Knowledge

As the Roman Empire collapsed and the Dark Ages began, all the wisdom and knowledge that had been part of that empire was lost to Western Europe.

Nevertheless, for the most part, that ancient knowledge and wisdom did survive through the centuries of the Dark Ages. It survived because of the Islamic empire that lay to the south and east of Europe.

By the end of the ninth century the internal struggles and divisions within Islam had settled down. The ruling Caliphs instituted a House Of Wisdom in Baghdad. Here they collected ancient Greco/Roman (Greek) and Indian (Sanskrit) texts, and brought in scholars who could read and understand them. This creative milieu lasted until the fourteenth century.

Greek, Roman, Persian and Indian texts, going back a thousand years, were preserved and translated into Arabic. Their content was studied and developed by Muslim scholars. Eventually this information was translated from Arabic to Latin.

These translations into Latin gave a kick-start to the resurgence of learning in Western Europe, known as the

Renaissance. They would eventually be the source of the ancient pagan philosophies for Christian Theologians.

The period from the ninth to the fourteenth century is sometimes called the Golden Age of Islam. By taking a look at the development of just two areas, mathematics and philosophy, we can get a glimpse of how the ancient knowledge was preserved and developed during this Golden Age.

Mathematics

In ancient Greece, Pythagoras (580 BC – 500 BC) was famous as a Philosopher and Mathematician. We all remember from our school days that, thanks to Pythagoras, 'the sum of the squares on the two sides is equal to the square of the hypotenuse'.

Another famous Greek was Archimedes, the greatest of ancient mathematicians, who contributed many of the concepts upon which higher mathematics depends.

Then, in 300 BC, there was Euclid known as the Father of Geometry. Amazingly, his book *Elements* was the main textbook used to teach geometry until the late nineteenth century.

This theoretical information produced some amazing practical results; amazing to us in the twenty-first century because we sometimes fail to understand what an important role science and technology played in the ancient world.

The picture of the world at the time of Christ as understood by many Christians is one where complex ideas and mechanisms are unknown. This picture is often reinforced by Hollywood's images and local nativity plays where the wardrobe consists of bathrobes, towels and sandals.

A good example that refutes this view is the *Antikythera Mechanism* that was made around 150 BC. It was recovered from an underwater wreck in the Mediterranean and is now in a museum in Athens.

The mechanism is an astronomical analogue calculator, or *Orrery*, and was used to predict the positions of celestial bodies. It is the oldest known complex scientific calculator – sometimes called the first analogue computer. The device has over thirty gears and is remarkable for the complexity of its parts. There was nothing comparable to it until the clocks of the seventeenth century.

There are many examples of this type of ancient knowledge that were preserved and developed within Islam. One of the products of the *House of Wisdom*, founded in AD 850, was the *Book of Ingenious Devices*. It contained details of over 100 mechanical gadgets from both the ancient and their contemporary world.

The way we write numbers today came from that time. When we write the price of something, for example £15.30, we know that each column represents values of zero to nine. This is known as the *place-value decimal system* and it can be traced back to ancient India.

An Arab mathematician, Al-Khwarizmi, wrote a book on the subject and when it was translated into Latin three hundred years later it became the major source for Europeans wanting to learn the new system. Al-Khwarizmi's algebra book was translated from Arabic into Latin in 1145 and it became very influential. So much so, that the Arabic phrase *al jabr*, in the book's title, is the reason we use the word "algebra" today.

Philosophy

European interest in Muslim philosophy began at the end of the eleventh century. One notable contributor was Al Farabi (AD 900), who made contributions in the field of Philosophy as well as in Logic, Mathematics, Medicine, Psychology and Music.

Following him came Ibn Sina (AD 981-1037), who was an eminent figure in Islamic science and one of the most famous exponents of *Muslim Universalism,* which influenced western thinking on Universalism. Even though he was a devout Muslim he sought to reconcile the rational philosophy of Aristotle with Islamic theology. He aimed to use reason and logic to scientifically prove the existence of God and his creation of the world. For a thousand years he has retained his original renown as one of the greatest thinkers in history. Of his surviving treatises, 150 concentrate on philosophy and 40 of them concentrate on medicine.

Ibn Sina was very influential upon the West. His influence, particularly with regard to Platonic philosophy, was felt through the Latin translation of his works done in the eleventh century, and also through the works of Jewish philosopher, Solomon ibn Gabirol, known as *Avencebrol,* who also promoted Neo-Platonism.

They influenced Thomas Aquinas, who shaped the Christian Theological thought of that time, and his major work, *The Sum of Theology* is still read today. The Roman Catholic Church considers Thomas Aquinas to be one of their greatest theologians and philosophers.

In 1210 and 1215, the Church prohibited the teaching of Aristotle's interpretations and Ibn Sina's books, but by the end of the fifteenth century the extensive printing and publication of books translated from Arabic into Latin, made the decree ineffective.

3: Development

During this time, many students from Southern France and Italy journeyed to the Islamic schools. They went to study mathematics, philosophy and medicine. In time, these same students became the leaders in the first Western universities.

Among the first universities to be founded in the thirteenth century were those of Paris, Bologna, Montpellier and Oxford. The leading center for translation and interpretation of the ancient texts was Oxford University.

The translation was often done in two stages, starting with a Jewish scholar living in Muslim Spain, who translated from the Arabic to a common language. A European scholar would then translate it into Latin.

By the thirteenth century, Reason (Philosophy) had become independent of Theology and begun to be studied as a separate subject.

In 1220, Frederick II, a German King and a great admirer of Muslim thought, was crowned the Emperor of Rome. In 1224 he established a university at Naples, which did much to introduce Muslim philosophy and science to the people of the West.

The parting of the ways between Theology and Philosophy, during the fourteenth and fifteenth centuries, resulted in many bitter debates, which still go on today.

These debates that once focused on Neo-Platonism and Aristotelian philosophy, now concern themselves with Marx (Liberation Theology) and Post Modernism.

The Islamic empire rescued, maintained, and to some extent developed the knowledge of the ancient world. However, it was in Christian Western Europe that these ideas and concepts were developed more fully.

Algebra was used to develop calculus, linear algebra, graphs, and matrices. Algorithms have been taken and used to develop electronics, digital computing, computers, robots, and the Internet.

Today we have Quantum Mechanics, Theories of Relativity, Cosmology and modern Astronomy, all of which help us to understand the marvels of the universe we live in. All of these have their roots in the mathematics that were birthed in the ancient world.

These same ancient sources, preserved in the Islamic empire, have shaped many of the philosophical and theological concepts in our modern society. However, many of these concepts run counter to the fundamental truths of the early Christian church.

The early church was formed from Holy Spirit led egalitarian groups, who were firmly rooted in Judaism. This shaped their view of God; of Creation; of the Fall; of the need for a Kinsman Redeemer; of the coming of the Messiah; and of the afterlife.

However, as time passed the ancient philosophical and theological concepts derived from the pagan world, began to take root in Christendom. This only became possible because of some major changes that took place in the way the Church lived out the Good News.

The first of these changes was the development of what is termed, the *episcopal system* of church governance.

CHAPTER TEN
The Episcopal System

The Episcopal System is a hierarchical form of church governance. It decrees that the chief authority over a local Christian church is a Bishop (Greek: *episcopos*). In some denominations the title Bishop is not used, but the hierarchical principle remains.

It is a feature of the Roman Catholic, Episcopal/Anglican and Methodist churches of today, and surprisingly, a feature of many of the so-called non-denominational 'free churches'. The episcopal form of church governance has its roots in the early days of the church, but not in the earliest.

At the council meeting in Jerusalem, chaired by James and as reported in Acts ch.15, it was agreed that the Gentiles were part of God's redemptive plan. As time passed, there was an ever-increasing number of ekklesia groups around the Roman Empire, many being predominantly Gentile. These were all were based on the egalitarian Jewish synagogue model.

The influence exerted by the core Judaic community waned as Christianity spread further afield throughout the empire. Even before the original first hand witnesses died, other ideas and conclusions about God, and the person of Jesus, began to circulate among the wider based Christian community.

These ideas posed a real challenge to the early church. The church of today has the advantage and sometimes the disadvantage - of 2,000 years of theological debate regarding the basics of faith.

The early church relied on experiential events and Holy Spirit led people. They had yet to develop precise definitions of what was the truth of their new life in Christ, and what was not. Variations of interpretation abounded.

One interpretation reflected the beliefs of Gnosticism. Gnosticism said that humans are divine souls trapped in a material world that had been created by an imperfect spirit. The way out from this is to get gnosis, or divine esoteric (secret), knowledge. In their letters to the ekklesia, both Paul and John warned against this teaching.

The teachings of Marcion, (he was subsequently excommunicated) were another challenge to the early church. He was so anti-Semitic that he did away with the Old Testament and much of the New. He believed in dualism. He taught that the God of the Old Testament was evil and the God of the New Testament (but only certain parts of it) was Good.

There was a reaction to this free flow of ideas, many of which were contrary to the orthodoxy of revealed truth. In order to protect the scattered ekklesia against these heresies, the Church centralized its power in the bishops. Using the Roman Empire as their model, they established a hierarchical organization with varying levels of authority. This was done in an effort to maintain orthodoxy.

Whereas the affairs of the first century church were directed by a group of elders who were also called bishops or overseers, the churches were now under the control of a single individual for whom the title bishop was reserved exclusively. Also at this time, the bishops began to be looked upon as the successors of the apostles.[xvi]

Nevertheless there was a continuing debate as to what constituted Christian orthodoxy and what did not. Arius (AD 250 – 330), said that God the Father and Jesus did not exist together eternally. He said that the Jesus was a divine being created by (and therefore inferior to) God the Father. This is known as Arianism and today the Jehovah's Witnesses espouse this same false teaching.

In AD 325, Constantine exercised his political power and organized the Council of Nicea. All the voting members were bishops, and the majority of them opposed Arius, so Arius was defeated and the issue was resolved. The Nicene Creed became the orthodox position on the deity and pre-existence of Jesus.

Constantine later reinstated Arius, and two of the following emperors, Constantine's son, Constantius II, and Valens, also promoted Arianism. As a result, Arianism continued to spread and to cause division in the Church during the remainder of the fourth century. This is a perfect example of how the kingdoms of men try to influence and change the kingdom of God.

This system that vested authority in the bishops, the *episkopoi*, is the foundation of the episcopal model of church governance with us to this day.

The simplest form of episcopal governance is found in the Methodist Church, which has only one level of bishops. Somewhat more developed is the governmental structure of the Anglican or Episcopal Church, while the Roman Catholic Church has the most complete system of hierarchy, with authority being vested especially in the supreme pontiff, the bishop of Rome, the Pope.[xvii]

It is important to understand that this system is not the 'God ordained' model that some claim it to be. It was designed and implemented for very practical reasons. It was a necessary defense mechanism needed at a time when the revealed truth of the Gospel was being undermined by various traveling teachers and so called 'apostles'.

This is not to say that God hasn't used it to good effect, he has. But this hierarchical organizational structure of church governance was not in the original blueprint for the church.

It is a man made stone added to the structure that only required a cornerstone, Jesus Christ.

There are those who support the episcopal form of church governance by using the historical argument that says there is a line of direct descent from the apostles to the bishops of today.

Ordination is seen as the means by which the apostle's authority is transferred through the centuries from one person to another.

In the New Testament, various people are said to have laid hands on others, but nowhere is it expressly stated that this laying on of hands conferred some kind of divine power of ordination.

> *Further, advocates of the episcopal form of church government give insufficient attention to Christ's direct exercise of lordship over the church. He installed Paul without any intermediary; no other apostle was involved. Paul makes much of this point when justifying his apostleship (Gal. 1: 15-17). Now if Paul received his apostleship directly from God, might not others as well? In other words, in at least this one case apostolic authority does not seem to rest on previous apostolic authority'.* [xviii]

The hierarchical, authoritarian, episcopal governance position is also weakened when we consider what Jesus taught about authority, and the way his followers should exercise it.

> *"But Jesus called them unto him, and said. 'Ye know that the princes of the Gentiles exercise dominion **over** them, and they that are great exercise authority upon them. But **it shall not be so among you.** but whosoever will be great among you let him be your minister;"(Matt 20:25-26, KJV) [The word translated here as minister is the Greek word diakonos - servant]*

> *"And he said unto them. 'The kings of the Gentiles exercise lordship **over** them; and they that exercise authority upon them are called benefactors. But **ye shall not be so.** but he that is greatest among you, let him be as the younger; and he that is chief, as he that doth serve". (Luke 22:25-26, KJV).*

'Dominion over', and 'lordship over' are from the Greek word "*katakurieuo*". The word is used to express the concept of 'rulership or authority over others', as being the defining aspect of **human** government.

Jesus specifically says here, that this is **not** the way it should be within the new covenant church.

In fact, these statements of Jesus rule out anyone exercising authority, over anyone else - under any circumstances! Jesus said, 'But ye shall not be so'.

Jesus defines 'leadership' as being a 'servant' to all. This is entirely the opposite of having authority over others in the way that worldly governments have.

Jesus goes on to say, "And he that is chief, as he that doth serve". The word translated as 'chief', is "*hegeomai*". Jesus specifically defines "hegeomai", or 'chief' as one being 'of service', to others.

However, there is a verse in 1Thessalonians that is often quoted, and appears to say the opposite of what Jesus says in the gospels of Matthew and Luke.

*"And we beseech you, brethren, to know them which labor among you, and are **over** you in the Lord, and admonish you;* "(1Thessalonians 5:12)

The word translated here, as "over", is the Greek word *"proistemi"* and this is the only place in the New Testament where it is translated as 'over'. It also occurs in I Timothy 3: 4,5; 5:17; Romans 12:8 and Titus 3:8, 14.

The phrase, *"proistemai tinos"*, means, "care for", "give aid to". It carries the sense of 'presiding over activities in an official capacity.' Greco-Roman people accepted the compatibility of benevolent care and structured authority.

The word that **does** mean 'to rule over' or 'to exercise authority over another' in the way that the world does, is "katakurieuo" as used in Matthew 20:25 or Luke 22:25.

This is different to the Greek word *"Proistemi"*. Therefore, a more correct translation of I Thessalonians 5:12 is as follows:

Now we ask you, fellow believers, to observe those among you who go to trouble for you, those you have chosen to care for you as the Lord's followers, those who warn you.[xix]

These people who are 'laboring among you' and 'are over you', are not actually to 'rule' over you'. In line with Jesus' statements they are the servants of God who are **caring** for the people, and with whom they should cooperate and help and seek to be like.

Within this concept of the exercise of authority within the church, we have the word 'submission'. The Greek word for submit or submission is *hupotasso*. In the forty times it is used, the word *hupotasso* is in the context of submitting to God; submitting to earthly authorities and within the husband and wife relationship. It is used **only once** in a context that can be interpreted as having to do with the authority of one believer over another.

Despite all of the above, we have to recognize that the Episcopal form of church governance plays a major role in the Christianity as practiced in the twenty-first century. Under other names it can be seen in the so-called 'free' churches.

Wherever there is a hierarchical structure, Senior Pastor, Assistant Pastor, leaders of this or that sub group then the episcopal system of church governance is present. It is even present in the small single pastor church because the desire to grow and expand along the lines of the accepted model is ever present.

There are innumerable 'bishops' or 'pastors' of every order who are truly servants to the flock and to Christ. Criticism of a system does not necessarily become criticism of the individuals trapped within it.

As stated earlier, the purpose of this book is to provide the information that will enable the reader to differentiate between what is at the core and what is peripheral to the authentic Christian life. Nevertheless, the episcopal hierarchical system is yet another man-made stone added to the structure that only required a cornerstone, Jesus Christ.

CHAPTER ELEVEN
Enter the Greeks and the Clergy

The Episcopal System became established at a time when changes were taking place in the political make up and stability of the Roman Empire. At the same time the basic makeup of the early church was changing from being predominantly Jewish, to becoming predominantly Gentile. The new Gentile leaders brought many new ideas in with them.

The siege and later destruction of Jerusalem as described in chapter 7, led to the center of Judaism moving from Jerusalem to Galilee and beyond into Babylon and Alexandria.

As a result, by the early years of the second century, the Christian ekklesia had changed from being a Jewish sect, based in the Jewish culture and with an all-Jewish leadership to becoming a separate 'religion', based in the Greco/Roman culture of the Empire, and with a mainly Gentile leadership.

By looking at the church at Corinth, we can catch a glimpse into the life and culture within which these Christian communities were formed. Paul's first letter to the Corinthians tells us a lot, even though it was written around AD 55. Corinth was a large cosmopolitan city and a *coloniae civium romanorum,* or a colony of Roman citizens, mainly because many military veterans had settled there with their families. A 'Rome away from Rome' so to speak.

Each person in the Corinthian group of believers had had a life changing personal experience of the risen Lord Jesus. Each one had been born again. Each one had been filled with the Holy Spirit. Each one evidenced one or more of the gifts of the Spirit, including speaking in tongues.

However, each one had come into the ekklesia from life on the outside. They may have been a temple prostitute, or a member of one of the many Hellenic societies that met to drink and party, or a member of a religious group that performed in a way totally at odds to the Judaic basis of the Christian group. Consequently they dressed and acted according to their own personal standard of what they considered to be 'normal'.

What was normal for them? We see that the Corinthian ekklesia included people following this or that famous teacher and who formed groups or factions. One of them was openly committing incest, others were suing each other in court, and some of them were going with harlots. Others were getting drunk during their meetings, and much more.

It was chaotic, and the churches in every area of the empire were no different. They all had problems of one sort or another, just as we do today. It was in trying to bring order to this chaotic mix that Paul wrote his letters of advice and instructions.

As mentioned previously, priests of that day did not give moral instruction; this came from philosophers and teachers. Only within the Judaic/Christian mind-set were morality and religion intertwined. This separation of religion and morality seems strange to us today, but it needs to be understood, especially when reading some of the moral instructions contained in the epistles.

Many of Paul's statements are the cause of contention among Christians today. Taking any one of them at its face value is to miss the point entirely. Everything in the New Testament is anchored firmly in the culture and context of the time and the place. Much of what we see practiced in the contemporary church is built on oversimplification, and just plain ignorance, of the cultural and contextual content of the New Testament writings.

In time the demographics of the ekklesia began to change. More and more people who had been raised in the Hellenic tradition and schooled in Greek philosophy, converted to Christianity. Many of them became influential leaders, and many were virulently anti-Semitic. For example, John Chrysostom (344-407 A.D.) said that a synagogue was worse than a brothel.

They also brought the philosophy and ideas of Plato with them, and these became interwoven with the Judaic roots from which Christianity had sprung.

Plato believed, among other things, in dualism. That is, that the spiritual realm is 'good' and the physical is 'evil'. On the other hand, despite sin being in the world, Judaism viewed all the creation as 'good' because God had declared it so.

It was through the influence of the Church Fathers that Christian Dualism, based on Platonic Dualism, became part of the church's mind-set.

At first Christians celebrated communion in their homes but in AD 110, as a result of this dualistic thinking, Ignatius said that the administering of the Holy Communion is valid only if there is a bishop present. The ordinary people could no longer share in the physical elements of the bread and the wine. These 'earthly' physical elements had to be 'spiritualized' by someone ordained for that purpose.

We still see this type of thinking at work in many churches today where things are ritualistically prayed over to make them 'holy' or certain places or objects are declared to be 'holy'.

Church Fathers like Origen, Justin and Clement, emphasized withdrawal from the world (the bad), to concentrate on 'spiritual' matters (the good). This was the root from which the separation of clergy (kleros) from laity (laos) began.

There is no suggestion in the New Testament Scriptures that the *kleros* are a class or group of persons distinct from the *laos*. The Greek word 'kleros' originally meant 'called' and the Greek word 'laos' meant 'people' - the people of God. So originally the 'kleros' were the 'laos' and the 'laos' were the 'kleros'.

The creation of a distinct group called clergy, who were separate from the laity, was accelerated by the teachings of Church Fathers, Tertullian and Cyprian and the idea that these clergy were more holy than the laity.

The original method of teaching was a dialogue in the rabbinical pattern, which allowed room for discussion and counter points. This was replaced by the Greek method of teaching that is in the style of a lecture. This Greek influence is still with us today. For example Christian seminaries and Bible colleges today teach:

Homiletics: (the art of writing and preaching sermons). This was influenced by another church father, John Chrysostom.

Hermeneutics: (the science and methodology of interpreting Biblical texts).

Oratory: Eloquence in public speaking, especially of the kind that shows the speaker's rhetorical skills.

It seems that today every successful priest or pastor needs to excel in these skills that are rooted in the pagan Hellenic system.

In transferring our dependence from mutual ministry with each other, to dependence on a lone pastor, we have made it to be a requirement to possess skills in oratory.

Humanism, which can be seen in so many aspects of our culture today, says that ethics and morality can change depending on what man reasons them to be. Humanism is yet another direct result of the input from the Platonic school of thought.

The effect of this institutionalization of the church as a whole and the influx of Hellenistic philosophies was to set the ekklesia at odds with the presence and leading of the Holy Spirit in all believers.

A consistent theme, running through all the centuries of the history of the ekklesia, is this divergence between the Holy Spirit filled people, who exhibit the gifts of the Spirit, and those who do not. The history of the church is the history of the Holy Spirit and the believers who make up the body of Christ.

Again we have seen how another man-made stone has been added to the original church structure. This time it is the influence of pagan Hellenic philosophical ideas (at this stage mainly from Plato) that were at odds to the revealed truth and practice of the church up to that point. The only stone that God's blueprint required was the cornerstone, Jesus Christ.

The next chapter explores how the increasingly institutionalized church dealt with the freedom that the Holy Spirit had brought.

CHAPTER TWELVE.
Institution And Spirit

The institutionalization of the church, which began in the second century and is still with us today, did help to stem the influence of heretical teachers. The references to Marcion, and to the Gnostics, in chapter ten, are good examples of the ideas against which the church had to defend itself at that time. The downside was that this same institutionalization opposed the freedom and the spiritual life that the Holy Spirit brought.

Findlay B Edge, one time professor of theological education at the Southern Baptist Theological Seminary put it rather well:

"Religion becomes institutionalized when its adherents are related primarily to the church as an institution or to the organizations of the church rather than to the living God. The religious life manifested is not the free and open outworking of a deep, spiritual relationship with God. Rather, in institutionalized religion the primary expression of a person's religion is that he supports the organization by his attendance; he supports the organization by his gifts; and in general he merely lives a "good" life."[xx]

The organization, and those holding offices within it, began to become more important than the vital new life in the Spirit. In the beginning, those who performed the various functions within the church were recognized by the fact that the Holy Spirit had given them the gift(s) required to perform that function. As institutionalization took over, those functions became offices that were filled by those who were loyal supporters of the organization, whether the Holy Spirit gifted them or not.

This meant that outward ecclesiastical forms of both office and ritual came to be valued over personal spiritual experiences. It also meant that spontaneous manifestations of the Holy Spirit became less and less desirable, especially by those in authority.[xxi]

A typical example of the reaction against the spontaneity of the Holy Spirit is to be found in the history of the Montanists. This movement, which began around AD 172 was named after its founder, Montanus. He said that the criterion for ministry in the church was possession of the gifts of the Holy Spirit, not the appointment to an office. His followers called themselves 'The New Prophecy' because their activities majored on the prophetic.

The movement became widespread throughout the Empire and Tertullian, one of the church fathers joined the Montanists in AD 2000. Although they had a lot of support from many of the influential leaders, reaction varied and there was also great opposition.

Those who believed that the holder of an ecclesiastical office had pre-eminence over someone who had a spiritual gift made their opposition known. They focused on the seemingly out-of-control way that the prophetic words were delivered and said this proved that the Montanists were demon possessed.

Because of the increasing opposition, another influential leader of the time, Irenaeus, had to intercede to the bishop of Rome on behalf of the Montanists.

However, the opposition won the day, and by the time of the Council of Constantinople in AD 381, the Montanists were declared heretics. History is written by the winners, and that is why in books on church history, so many references to the Montanists refer to them in the light of that decision and ignore their previous history.

There are two Greek words for 'another'; the first is *allos*, which means *another of the same sort,* (e.g. I have an apple and ask for an allos piece of fruit - you should give me an apple) the second word is *heteros*, which means *another of a different sort,* (you can give me a pear or an orange).

In the fourteenth chapter of John's Gospel, Jesus promised to send "**another** Comforter" once he left the earth. Jesus used the word allos, which means that the Holy Spirit is the same as Jesus. In John chapters 14 to 16, Jesus refers to the Holy Spirit, and he uses the personal pronoun (he/him) a total of eighteen times.

The church was birthed at Pentecost and only exists where the Holy Spirit (Jesus) is present and active. Whenever the church is operating without the Holy Spirit's active presence it will, despite all its good intentions and deeds, deteriorate into being just one more secular organization.

Over the centuries the Holy Spirit has manifested his presence and power in quite diverse ways. From time to time the response of some was to go well beyond what the Spirit was intending. In reaction to those excesses, many others then denied the Spirit's presence and power and so frustrated what he intended.

There were also attempts to control the Holy Spirit; an example being the 'Roman Ritual', published in AD 1000. It said that if the common people spoke in tongues they were demon possessed. However, at the same time, it was understood that if a member of the church hierarchy spoke in tongues, it was a sign of sainthood.

One of the groups who came into conflict with the institutional church, were the Cathari. This was the name given to various groups of Christians who believed in the Bible and operated in the gifts of the Holy Spirit.

As with the Montanists, their history was written by those who suppressed and overcame them. One group of Cathari was based in the town of Albi in France and were known as Albigensians.

Bernard Gui, an Inquisitor of the Dominican Order, wrote of them in his, "On The Albigensians".

> *"... they usually say of themselves that they are good Christians, ... hold the faith of the Lord Jesus Christ and his gospel as the apostles taught ... occupy the place of the apostles.... ...they talk to the laity of the evil lives of the clerks and prelates of the Roman Church... ... they attack and vituperate, in turn, all the sacraments of the Church, especially the sacrament of the Eucharist, saying that it cannot contain the body of Christ... Of baptism, they assert that the water is material and corruptible ... and cannot sanctify the soul... ... they claim that confession made to the priests of the Roman Church is useless... They assert, moreover, that the cross of Christ should not be adored or venerated... Moreover they read from the Gospels and the Epistles in the vulgar tongue, applying and expounding them in their favor and against the condition of the Roman Church..."*

The Cathari who survived the bloody massacres and who weren't burned at the stake were put on trial and charged with heresy. At their trials many of them referred to the Bible and quoted from it in their defense.

As a result, in 1292, the Synod of Toulouse forbade the laypeople from reading the Bible in their own common language. In order to provide an effective barrier to keep the people from reading the Bible and learning the truth for themselves, an edict was passed ordering that the Scriptures be kept in Latin only – the language of the priests and scholars.

In the twelfth century, the Waldenses, another group who operated in the gifts of the Holy Spirit were excommunicated just like the Cathari. They continued until the early sixteenth century when they were absorbed into the Reformation. The Waldensian church still exists today, but in a modified form.

In 1382, John Wycliffe published the Bible in English. He challenged many of the doctrines and practices of the organizational church at that time. After his death he was declared a heretic and his bones were dug up and burned.

His followers, known as Lollards, were persecuted, but as with the Waldenses, they were eventually absorbed by the Reformation.

One famous Lollard was Sir John Oldcastle, a great friend of King Henry V (of Agincourt fame). The friendship was not enough to save him, and he was eventually hanged and then burned at the stake. It is said that William Shakespeare based the fictional character of Sir John Falstaff on Sir John Oldcastle.

The great upheaval of the Reformation did nothing to change the conflict between the organized hierarchical church and those who lived in response to the Holy Spirit. Both the Lutherans and the Roman Catholics persecuted the Anabaptists; a group who believed in adult baptism following conversion by the Holy Spirit, rather than infant baptism that they said accomplished nothing.

What the Reformation did do though, was to allow these dissident groups (both good and bad) to exist outside of the ruling groups, the ones who exercised authority and influence in the world.

Many groups with whom we are familiar today, and many not so familiar, such as the Mennonites, the Quakers, the Camisards, the Moravians and the Methodists, had their beginnings in a charismatic move of the Holy Spirit. As has often proved to be the case, most of these developed into, and are now firmly established as hierarchical, institutional organizations.

The Holy Spirit moved within and across the denominations too. The First Great Awakening (1726 - 1750) and the Second Great Awakening (1800 - 1840), touched many people in all denominations and all walks of life. Many of the famous American colleges and universities of today such as Princeton and Columbia were founded in response to these great moves of the Holy Spirit.

The Holiness Movement, and then the Azuza Street revival in 1906, birthed the mainline Pentecostal and Evangelical churches of today.

The Charismatic movement that spread throughout the mainline denominations beginning in the 1950's, is yet another example of how the Holy Spirit still perseveres to maintain his presence in the church.

The struggle between the institutions and the Holy Spirit still continues unabated. Despite two thousand years of interaction and witness by the Holy Spirit, the institutionalization of the church is a repeating pattern.

The original church, the ekklesia, were small relational groups of Holy Spirit filled people, who deferred to each other in respect to the individual gifting by the Holy

Spirit. These groups were connected to each other in a loose and informal fellowship.

The unifying factor was that they had all been born-again by the life-giving Spirit of God; evidenced his presence by his gifts, and had fellowship with the risen and ever-living Jesus Christ. They were living out that transformed life as best they could in the world they lived in. They depended totally on the Holy Spirit to guide them and see them through. This is the essence of the authentic Christian life.

Do the authoritarian hierarchical organizations that make up so much of the church today help or hinder this process? Is the word of God, the Scriptures, deferred to as the ultimate authority, or is it the traditions of men that provide the yardstick? Is the Holy Spirit seen to be at work equally among the members, or is he seen to be the prerogative of only a few?

These are issues that have been at the heart of the Christian way for twenty centuries. The questions posed need to be answered by every generation. With respect to our own individual walk with the Lord, each one of us needs to answer these and similar questions. The answers we get, and our response to them, will determine whether we move toward a more authentic Christian life or not.

This struggle between the Holy Spirit who wants to bring freedom, and the institutions who want to impose restrictions, is just one of the many influences that have been at work in the development of the church. This rejection and suppression of the Holy Spirit is yet another man-made stone and adds to the man-made edifice that will one-day crumble and fall, leaving only one stone standing--the cornerstone--Jesus Christ.

In the next chapter we will look at some familiar, but nevertheless, important 'stones' that shape the way we do church today.

CHAPTER THIRTEEN
Church Buildings, Liturgy and the Sermon

As mentioned at the beginning of this book, a first century Christian convert would recognize most of what we accept as normal in the way we do church in the 21st century. The issue here is that he would recognize them all as being pagan. He would probably flee the place in order to preserve who he was in Christ Jesus.

The first of the man-made stones that was added to the cornerstone, Jesus Christ, came about by the imposition of a hierarchical episcopal system of governance. This effectively quenched the Holy Spirit and replaced him and his gifts with offices filled by officers loyal to the hierarchical organization. The church 'building' began to move out of alignment from the cornerstone.

The next man-made stone was the infusion of pagan Greek philosophical ideas. This further skewed the 'building' from its alignment with the cornerstone- Jesus and from God's blueprint. To repeat the statement of church father, Tertullian, "What has Athens to do with Jerusalem?" He clearly recognized the danger.

As we next look at the history of the church in the years leading up to the Reformation, we will see how other man-made stones were added. Stones that further moved the church from its true alignment with Jesus Christ, **the** cornerstone.

In AD 317, the emperor of the West (Constantine), and the emperor of the east (Licinius), issued the edict of Milan. From that time on, Christianity was accepted and in time operated hand in glove with the state.

One effect of the Constantine 'conversion' was that Christians started to have their own special buildings. These formed an ideal setting for the development of institutional rituals and liturgical practices; rituals and practices that were absent from the foundational ekklesia or early church.

1: Buildings

The institution had created 'offices' each with its own function. These functions gradually changed in order to fit the changes in the institutional practices. For example, by the third century the presbyters, or elders who were *assistants* to the bishop in the second century, had become priests (Latin sacerdos).

The Roman culture embraced all religions as long as they put the Emperor first. All these religions, with the exception of Christianity, had their own special buildings.

Judaism was no exception. The temple in Jerusalem contained the Kodesh Hakodashim (Hebrew for the Holy of Holies). It was the place where God dwelt. Only the Kohen Gadol (high Priest) could enter it. Sacrifices were made to offset the sins of the people. The sacrifice was known as a Korban ("to come close to God"). Korban was usually an animal sacrifice that underwent Shechita (Jewish ritual slaughter).

The Pagan temples of the time also had their own rituals. Some of the temples were as big as a football field and they were orientated toward the east. The central structure contained a statue of the god, it was known as the Naos (the place where god dwelt). Sacrifices, in one form or another, were normal practice. Most of these pagan temples were highly decorated with depictions of battles and other real or mythical events.

Christianity was rooted in Judaism. The surrounding Greco/Roman culture was filled with a variety of pagan religions, yet for the first 300 years of its existence the Christian church met in private homes, public spaces or commercial buildings. They did not have special buildings, priests or sacrifices. Why not?

Jesus became the once and for all sacrifice (Hebrews ch.10). He opened up the way into the Holy of Holies (Mark 15:38; Matthew 17:51 and Luke 23:45). Every believer is a dwelling place (naos) for the Holy Spirit (1 Corinthians 3:16) and every believer is part of the Royal Priesthood (1 Peter 2:9).

Therefore, for the early Christians, sacrifices, priests and temples were redundant.

They met in homes (Acts 2:46). Larger groups met in public places (Acts 5:12), or in larger private places (Acts 19:9). This pattern continued for over two hundred years, however, as time passed, the influence of the surrounding culture began to take effect.

The phrase "going to church' was first used by Clement (AD 150-215). Most believers of the day would have been puzzled. How can you go to what you are?

The Greek word *ekklesia*, usually translated as church, is a group of people. Actually the root of the English word 'church' comes from the Greek word *kuriakom*, meaning 'belonging to the Lord'.

The Christians began to gradually absorb the pagan idea of special places being sacred. This came about in part from the reverence they gave to the tombs of martyrs, and they would sometimes use these special places as a meeting place. Markers were erected to signify that these places were held in special regard. This set the scene for what happened after Constantine's conversion.

Constantine encouraged the building of special buildings on these special sites. These buildings were based on the design of the government buildings, known as *Basilicas*, and the design of the basilica was based on the design of the pagan temple.

The fourth century 'Christian' buildings exerted a major influence and changed the way the church developed. Many of the practices carried out in the official buildings, and in pagan temples, were incorporated into the practices within the new church buildings. (See Appendix One).

The architecture of church buildings changed with the years. The fourth century Byzantine buildings had central domes and ornate decoration. The ninth century Romanesque had large pillars and round arches. The most impressive of these church buildings are the great Gothic style cathedrals from the twelfth century on.

Architectural innovations, such as the pointed arches, ribbed vaults and flying buttresses, enabled these buildings to be taller, wider and grander than any before. They took generations to build. It has been said that a higher proportion of the gross national product (GDP) was used to build these great cathedrals, than that utilized by the USA in the Apollo program that put a man on the moon.

The massive outlay on buildings continues to this day. A church in Texas leased a redundant sports facility and then spent $75,000,000.00 on refurbishment and redesign.

They later purchased it outright for a further $7,500,000.00. This is not an isolated case.

It is estimated that the real estate owned by the Christian church in the USA today, is worth 230 billion dollars. Around ten billion of the fifty to sixty billion dollars tithed annually into churches is spent on buildings, servicing the debt and maintenance.[xxii]

So why do we feel the need to spend such vast sums on buildings? The answer is of course; without these buildings we would not be able to carry out the ritual of the weekly service. This ritual, for the most part carried out on a Sunday, is for many Christians, what church is all about. When they walk in the door they know what to expect.

2: The Liturgy

It was the same in the ancient world. Every group or cult, who favored a particular god or gods, had its own format of expected ritual. From simple private acts, to complex and lengthy ceremonies, each person knew what was expected of them.

When the early Christians gathered together they too had an expectation of each other and of God, but no set format or ritual:

*How is it then brethren? When you come together, **every one of you** has a psalm, a doctrine, has a tongue, has a revelation, and has an interpretation. Let all things be done unto edifying.* (1 Corinthians 14:26 - Emphasis mine)

*Let the word of Christ dwell in you richly in all wisdom, teaching and admonishing **one another** in psalms and hymns* *and spiritual songs, singing with grace in your hearts to the Lord.* (Colossians 3:16. - Emphasis mine).

*And when they had prayed, the place was shaken where they were assembled together; and they were all filled with the Holy Spirit, and **they** spoke the word of God with boldness.* (Acts 4:31. - Emphasis mine)

It is clear that there was a freedom for every one of them to express themselves as the Holy Spirit led. It was spontaneous, unplanned and not following a set order or program. They were in mutual ministry, one to another.

Compare that to the standard pattern followed every weekend in most Protestant churches worldwide. (see Appendix Two). I have personally witnessed this repeating pattern in places and cultures as far apart as Japan, Poland, England, Hong Kong, Thailand and the USA.

No matter which church you visit, and in whatever country you experience it, the weekly ritual tends to follow a common pattern and contains similar elements.

Another element that has undergone a series of fundamental changes is the "Lord's Supper".

"For the early Christians, the Lord's Supper was a festive communal meal. The mood was one of celebration and joy. When believers first gathered for the meal, they broke bread and passed it around. Then they ate the meal, which then concluded after the cup was passed round. The Lord's Supper was essentially a Christian banquet. And there was no clergyman to officiate."[xxiii]

Again we see that contemporary practice differs widely from the original.

The question is – If the stylized rituals we have today did not exist in the early New Testament church, where did they come from, and how did they get to be accepted as 'church practice'? The answer to that question has its beginnings in the early Middle Ages. Particularly with Pope Gregory the Great (AD 540–604).

Many revered him; hence his title 'the Great', but there were some aspects to his character that were not so great. He was a very superstitious man, and really believed that religious relics had spiritual powers and that they could heal people. He believed in pagan magic and he advocated a celibate priesthood, something that had been common in the pagan Greco/Roman world.

"The requirement (celibacy) was not one of morality, but of ritual purity, and the assigning of priesthoods to the very old or very young conforms to the ancient view that sexual functions were ceremonially defiling".[xxiv]

It was Gregory who, by blending pagan and Judaistic ritual, current church practices and theology of his day, developed the format of the Medieval Catholic Mass.

"In effect the Catholic Mass that emerged in the sixth century was fundamentally pagan. Christians incorporated the vestments of the pagan priests, the use of incense and holy water in purification rites, the burning of candles in worship, the architecture of the Roman basilica for their buildings, the law of Rome as the basis of canon law", the title Pontifex Maximus' for the head bishop, and the pagan rituals for the Catholic Mass"[xxv]

Transubstantiation is the changing of the bread or wafer and the wine, into the actual physical presence of Jesus Christ. It was central to the Medieval Mass, where Christ was sacrificed anew at each mass.

Neo-Platonism said that the physical was evil and the spiritual was good, therefore a special 'spiritual' person (a priest), vested with supernatural powers from God, and 'spiritual' words (the liturgy), was needed to transform the 'evil' elements into the 'holy' Eucharist.

This repetitious Christian 'sacrifice' of Jesus took place in the holy area of the church building. The design of the building and the sacrificial aspect, were based on the pagan rituals in the pagan temples. In the medieval mass we see at work several of the outside pagan influences that fundamentally changed the church.

But, you may ask, didn't the Reformation change all this? Yes, the Reformation did indeed bring about some fundamental changes. These changes are those on which the whole of the Protestant Church is founded, however, those changes were more to do with the theology of Christianity, rather than the form in which it was practiced.

The Reformation, which is reckoned to have started when Martin Luther nailed his ninety-five Theses on the church door in 1517, did not happen overnight.

About two hundred years prior to this event John Wycliffe, (1320 – 1384), had confronted the church with the Biblical truths. Many others followed, Jon Huss of Bohemia burned as a heretic in 1415, and Savonarola of Florence, also burned as a heretic in 1498, were just two of the many voices raised in protest.

It was from this turmoil of internal disputes (everyone was a Roman Catholic), and confrontation with the Church authorities that the leaders of the Reformation, Luther, Zwingli, Calvin, emerged. All of them put the emphasis on God's word (The Bible), rather than on the traditions of men.

In 1523 Luther revised the Catholic Mass.

"While Luther had a very high view of the Eucharist, he stripped the Mass of all sacrificial language, only keeping the Eucharist itself. He was a strong believer in both Word and Sacrament. So his German Mass assumed both holy communion and preaching."[xxvi]

Luther decreed that the liturgy was to be in the language of the people and not in Latin, which most could not understand. At Communion, both the bread and the wine were given to the people, and Christ was not re-sacrificed each time.

Most importantly, the Word and a preached sermon became the central focus rather than the living presence of the risen Christ in each believer.

Zwingli (1484 – 1531) said that the Lord's Supper was not taken every week, and the Altar became the Communion Table, and Calvin (1509 -1564) decreed that God was accessed through the preaching of the Word, not through the Eucharist. The preacher was the MC and CEO.

Although these changes represented a change in the theological understanding of man's relationship with God, and his relationship within the church, the template of the Medieval Mass remained as the foundation of the service.

The opportunity for radical reform, and a return to the original model for the ekklesia, was missed. That is why the Anabaptists of the time referred to Luther and Zwingli as "half way men".

From the time of the Reformation, and even right up to the present day, many influences have been at work to bring about changes to the order of worship.

In the sixteenth and seventeenth centuries the Puritans got rid of clerical robes and ornaments, and all closely followed a written liturgy. The Methodists of the eighteenth century brought in pre-sermon prayers that covered intercession, confession and praise. Later, with the invention of gaslight, they introduced the Sunday Evening service.

The frontier revivalists in the USA introduced another radical change.

*"They preached exclusively with one aim: to convert lost souls. ….. This emphasis finds it seeds in the innovative preaching of George Whitefield. He is the man who shifted the emphasis in preaching from God's plan for the church to God's plan for the individual".*xxvii

The use of music to generate emotional response, and altar calls, became the norm. They were pragmatic in their approach. 'If it works then do it' was their motto. The end was said to justify the means.

The modern Pentecostal movement began in Azusa Street in 1906. It gave the pew sitters freedom to dance or sing or clap their hands as the Spirit led, but the sermon was still retained as the focal point of the service.

3: The Sermon

For 500 years it has been the central part of the service, and for many churchgoers it is their sole source of spiritual food. However, it too is totally unscriptural, having its foundations in the pagan culture of the ancient world. (See Appendix Three).

In the early development of the church, it was the influential theologians, eminent Christian teachers and great bishops, collectively known as the Church Fathers, who exerted the greatest influence. Their scholarly works usually set a precedent for doctrine and practice.

For the most part these were men who, prior to their conversion to Christianity, had been raised and educated as pagans in the surrounding pagan culture. After conversion, the fruits of that pagan educational system remained with them. Of these, the art of rhetoric exercised the most influence.

> *"The most common form of advanced education, also available to one who entered a 'profession', was in rhetoric. It was something of the ancient equivalent of the college arts degree. We can hardly exaggerate the influence of rhetorical education on ancient culture and literature"*[xxviii]

Rhetoric can be traced back to the Sophists of the fifth century BC. They developed the art of persuasive argument, aimed more at winning the debate than presenting the truth. Aristotle in the third century BC made the statement that it all should have a beginning, middle and an end.

By the time of the early church, rhetoricians were highly thought of and highly paid. They were regarded in a similar way to how our modern culture admires its pop stars and, just like them, had groupies who followed them from venue to venue.

The intellectual and articulate Church Fathers followed this style, and in doing so encouraged the use of one-way monologues. This was in direct opposition to the mutual discussions that were at the heart of the early church groups. This change in style was aided by the way the church evolved into being a hierarchical, institutionalized structure.

John Chrysostom (from the Greek meaning 'golden mouthed') is the Church Father who was most influential in establishing the institution of the Christian sermon.

"The sermons were written down by the audience and subsequently circulated, revealing a style that tended to be direct and greatly personal, but was also formed by the rhetorical conventions of his time and place." [xxix]

When the Reformation in the sixteenth century changed the emphasis from the Eucharist to the Word, the pulpit replaced the altar table as the primary focus. For Luther the sermon was preeminent, thereby further enhancing its importance and centrality. Calvin used the sermon to systematically present the main doctrines from Scripture.

The Puritans of the seventeenth century developed a sermon style that was highly structured and gave a detailed verse-by-verse exposition. They also promoted a plainer and less intellectually demanding style of preaching.

The Great Awakening of the eighteenth century produced a more demonstrative style of presenting the sermon. The preacher would give way to strong outbursts of emotion, to screaming and to running up and down the platform.

Most of the above styles, from one extreme to the other, can be seen in a cross-section of the contemporary church. The common unifying factor is that the sermon, with its roots based in pagan practices, is the central component of the Christian order of service. In turn, this Christian order of service also has its roots in pagan liturgical practices, as does the layout of the church building it is performed in.

All of this is a far cry from the original church of the first century ekklesia. In summary we can see that:

- The format of the Catholic Mass was based on Judaic and pagan rituals.

- Protestant orders of service are based on the Catholic Mass.

- The Reformation changed the theology, but not the form.

- The Clergy still play the central role but with the sermon being the focal point rather than the Eucharist.

- The people are passive listeners and are not encouraged to minister to each other during the proceedings.

- Special buildings are required in order to accommodate all of the above.

All these, together with the format and content of the contemporary order of worship, have been revealed for what they are; man-made unscriptural stones that have been added to the cornerstone.

Man's tradition is an aberration, a moving away from the original, God-ordained model for his church. A model that was designed to be truly aligned with "the cornerstone", Jesus Christ.

The church of Jesus Christ should be the pillar and ground of truth, and not the defender of man's traditions.

Passivity inhibits God's requirement, which says specifically that we are to minister to one another. Lack of spontaneity due to the fixed order of service produces boredom and feeds passivity. To counteract this, pastors resort to, 'if it works do it' ideas which in turn lead to the introduction of even more unscriptural practices.

In their book, 'Pagan Christianity', Frank Viola and George Barna pose the following questions:

> "How can a man preach a sermon on being faithful to the Word of God while he is preaching a sermon? How can a Christian passively sit in a pew and affirm the priesthood of all believers when he is sitting passively in a pew? To put a finer point on it, how can you claim to uphold the Protestant doctrine of solar scriptura ("by the scripture only") and still support the pulpit sermons?[xxx]

The headship of Jesus Christ, and the influence of the Holy Spirit are reduced to the gifting and learning of one human being, the priest or pastor.

In the following chapter – we will look at the role and authority of the priest or pastor.

CHAPTER FOURTEEN
Priest/Pastor And Anointing

In the contemporary church the pastor may be the CEO, the teacher, the preacher, the one who has both spiritual and organizational authority, the caretaker, the fundraiser, the planner, the mainstay of all that happens, and anything else that is required.

In most churches the pastor is the *solar pastor* and performs most, and sometimes all, of these functions. What follows is not intended in any way to be a criticism of the men and women of God who labor so hard in the office of pastor or priest. It is just an explanation of how we came to have this 'office' in the first place.

We have seen that after the development of the hierarchical organization, came buildings, a set order of service, and a change of focus to the Eucharist and/or the sermon. In order to serve these purposes, functional positions were created.

The Eucharist, in particular, required a special person to carry out the necessary function. This special person occupied the office of priest/pastor.

The roles of priest and of pastor are mentioned in the New Testament. However, other than when referring to Jesus or to the Judaic priesthood, priest is mentioned only three times (Revelation 1:6; 5:10 and 20:6). At each one of those times it is a reference to *all* believers.

Pastor is only mentioned once (Ephesians 4:11) and then it is in the plural – pastors. Interestingly, snake handling is referred to twice (Mark.16: 18 and Acts.28: 3-6). This raises the question - can these minimal New

Testament references be used to support the office of priest/pastor, or even snake handler in the contemporary church?

Obviously since snake handling has not been adopted as regular church doctrine or ritual, the answer must be no. Nevertheless the office of pastor exists and we need to understand where it came from.

The changes leading to a hierarchical organizational structure; the influence of pagan converts and neo Platonism (spiritual is good and the physical is evil), together with a liturgy based on pagan practices, have been discussed earlier.

The result of these aberrations was the creation of the 'offices' of Bishops and Priests. They were tasked with serving the Eucharist and exercising spiritual authority over the flock. Thus denying the doctrine of the priesthood of all believers (1 Peter 2:9), and the fact of "Christ in us the hope of glory" (Colossians 1:27), all of which require that we need no mediator between man and God except Christ himself.

As the power and the influence of the church developed through the Middle Ages, it also grew great in possessions. Along with the ownership of great tracts of land and the resulting income, came political power and authority. Church and state worked hand in hand, but when a dispute arose the church generally won by using the threat of excommunication.

The social and political system of the High Middle Ages (1000 to 1300) is known as the "feudal system". Contrary to what most Christians believe, the practice of tithing in the church has its roots in this medieval feudal system, and not in the Old Testament Law.

Under the feudal system the nobles owned and held the land and allowed their vassals to live and work off it. In return, the vassal would fight for the noble and pay him a percentage of the income from the land. This was known as "the tithe".

Mainly due to the effects of the Black Death in the mid-fourteenth century, the medieval feudal system broke down, and came to an end. The Black Death killed off between thirty and sixty percent of the population of Europe, which in turn led to great changes in the social and economic order.

The feudal system had decreed that tenants tithed their income to the landowner. Even after the system ceased to exist, the church continued to exact the tithe from its tenants. Later, this became Canon Law and was extended to include everyone because, with the exception of Jews and Muslims, everyone in Europe was classed as being a Christian.

The early church, understanding that they were no longer subject to the Law, *did not* tithe. What they did do was to give freely and often far in excess of ten per cent. (Acts 4:34-37).

The Old Testament instituted three types of tithe:

1. Of the produce of the land to support the Levites, who had no inheritance in Canaan. (Lev.27:30-33; Num.18:21-30).

2. Of the produce of the land (could be converted to cash if having to travel) to support religious festivals. (Deut.14:22-27).

3. Of the produce of the land every third year, for the support of the Levites, widows, strangers and orphans. (Deut.14:28-29; 26:12-13)

As can be seen, a literal following of the Old Testament Law regarding tithing would exact twenty three and one third percent and not the measly ten per cent called for in the churches of today. Those who espouse tithing in the contemporary church do not preach this Biblical truth. If they did, they know that there would be a stampede for the door.

By the time of the Reformation the position and authority of the priests was unquestioned. The Reformers changed the theology but not the practice, and so the role of 'Pastor' or 'Presbyter' replaced that of priest. As John Milton put it in 1653, *"The new presbyter is but the old priest writ large"*. The brand name had changed, but the product, except for some minor changes, stayed the same.

The Reformers believed in ordination. The 'Ordination' ceremony has no scriptural basis, and is derived from pagan practices.

> *"The contemporary practice of ordination creates a special caste of Christian. Whether it be the priest in Catholicism or the pastor in Protestantism, the result is the same: The most important ministry is restricted to a few "special" believers. Such an idea is as damaging as it is unscriptural. The New Testament nowhere limits preaching, baptizing or distributing the Lord's Supper to the "ordained".* [xxxi]

However, the Reformers did draw the line at the idea of the pastor having special powers. What they did say was that the pastor, being specially educated for the task, was the mediator of God's will and word.

In the contemporary Protestant church, the Pastor is as powerful, if not more so, than a priest of the medieval church. The average pew-sitting Christian thinks that the Pastor is in a more privileged position to serve the Lord than they are. This reduces them to being second class Christians prevented from ministering to others during the meeting (1 Corinthians 12 – 14). This also prevents them from being able to carry out their priestly function (1 Peter 2). The pastor has replaced Jesus as the head of the ekklesia.

So why don't these God-fearing, Bible believing, committed Christians, who feel called to be pastors, not step down from that position? Why do they continue to prevent the church from functioning as the free, open, mutually participatory, every-member functioning body as described in the New Testament?

For the most part, the answer lies in their acceptance of the misplaced traditions of men and their belief that they have been especially anointed for the task.

Most people will agree, that the abuses of spiritual power, which we all abhor, seem to occur most readily, when the distinction between what is of God and what is of man, becomes blurred.

The subject of 'the anointing' carries with it a much used and abused terminology. There is a great deal said and taught about this in the contemporary church. Does the New Testament support some of the theories most commonly associated with this much-abused term, 'the anointing'? We shall see.

The starting point is to differentiate between 'organizational authority' and 'spiritual authority'. In any secular hierarchical organization, there has to be a top down exercise of management authority, otherwise there would be chaos. The same holds true for a church based on the hierarchical model. No matter the size of the church, the Pastor is the CEO and has to have the authority to manage.

The problem arises when this necessary secular authority is merged with spiritual authority. A commonly held view, is that spiritual authority is invested in a person, because that person has 'an anointing' from God. The logic being that when God speaks, his words are total authority, therefore, a person with a 'special' anointing also has God's authority. He or she can thus exercise that authority over other Christians who do not have that 'special' anointing'.

Is there some sort of 'mantle' placed by God upon a special person, which imbues them with God's authority over and above any other believer? If so, it would look somewhat similar to the example we have in Elijah and Elisha. When Elisha took Elijah's cloak, the spiritual power that Elijah had was seen to have passed to Elisha. (2 Kings. 2:14-15)

The Old Testament Hebrew word, *mishchah*, translated as 'anointing', obviously carries with it connotations to the New Testament Greek word, *chrisma*, also translated as anointing.

However, that was in the Old Testament times, when the Holy Spirit came to special people, at special times, for a special reason. Pentecost changed that. The Holy Spirit comes to all who believe. When referring to *all* born-again, Spirit-filled believers, in this post-Pentecost, New Testament time, the Bible tells us that we are *all* filled with the Holy Spirit, and that Christ lives in *all* of us:

> But **this** is that which was spoken by the prophet Joel; and it shall come to pass in those last days, saith God, that I will pour

out my Spirit on all flesh: and your sons and your daughters shall prophesy, and your young men shall see visions, and your old men shall dream dreams. And on my servants and on my handmaidens I will pour out in those days of my Spirit; and they shall prophesy. (Acts 2: 16 – 18)

Hereby know we that we dwell in Him, and He in us, because He has given us of His Spirit. (I John 4:13)

The Bible tells us that *"All the fullness of the Godhead is in Him"*, and that *'All power and authority in heaven and earth has been given to Him.'* The Bible also tells all the members of the Body of Christ, that we are His ambassadors.

Now an ambassador is invested with the ability to represent, speak for, act on behalf of, and carries the full weight of the authority of the country, or king that he or she represents. As ambassadors for Christ, we all have that authority invested in us by the indwelling presence of God, of the Christ and of the Holy Spirit.

*One Lord, one faith, one baptism, one God and Father of all, who is above all, and through all, and **in you all**.(Ephesians 4: 5-6)*

'In you all' is a phrase that in Greek, English or any other language, means what it says, "in you all." It clearly does not say, 'in some special people'. Nevertheless, there are many who would deny what the Bible clearly says, and they claim that only special people, (among whom they usually count themselves), have this indwelling 'special anointing.'

The reasonable conclusion that one can draw from what the Bible actually says is that the 'anointing', referred to by many in the church today, cannot be talking about the same anointing that Elijah had, nor can it be related to Elijah's mantle, simply because you cannot give something to a person if they already have it. The Bible says that *all* born-again believers already have it.

The word 'Anoint'.

Now a closer look at the word itself. What does the Bible, especially the post-Pentecost New Testament, say about anointing? The English word, 'anoint; anointing' is used fifteen times in the New Testament Scriptures.

Six times it is translated from: *aliepho, to oil with grease, fat, sumptuousness.* For example: *'anointed with oil many that were sick' (Mark 6:13)*

Twice it is translated from: *epichrio, to smear over.* For example: *'anointed the eyes of the blind man' (John 9:6)*

Seven times it is translated from: *chrisma☐ , to smear, to endow with;* or *chrio, to smear, to consecrate.*

Chrisma or Chrio – to endow or consecrate- is the obvious area to study. It is used only seven times, and we see that four of these seven times it refers specifically to Jesus alone.

This leaves only three remaining times when Chrio or Chrisma is used. One of these times it refers to Paul, and arguably, in that particular instance, to *all* the ekklesia at Corinth.

Now he that establishes us with you in Christ, and hath anointed (chrio) *us, is God. (II Corinthians 1:21)*

On the two remaining occasions, it specifically says that *all* believers have this anointing.

These things have I written to you concerning them that seduce you. But the anointing (chrio) *which you have received of him abideth in you, and ye need not that any man teach you: but as the anointing* (chrio) *teacheth you of all things, and is the truth, and is no lie, and even as it has taught you, ye shall abide in him. (I John 2: 26-27)*

The word, chrisma *endowment of* is also translated one time as 'unction' and in a verse addressed to *all* believers

But ye have an unction (chrisma), from the Holy One and know all things (I John 2 20)

It is clear from this brief study of the words *Chrisma* and *Chrio*, in the context of Pentecost and the coming of the Holy Spirit,' that *all* born-again believers have the 'anointing.

This begs the question as to what is the 'anointing' that many preachers/teachers in the church today refer to. What is this 'special anointing,' which is over and above the one the Bible speaks of?

Moreover, is there such a thing as a "double anointing"? I've heard some say, that in return for this or that, (usually money); they will ensure the donor will receive a 'double anointing.' Can this be true? Does this mean that some can have 100%, but others can have 200%? If Jesus Christ is, and has the fullness of God, he has 100%; and so do we because he indwells us.

For in Him (Jesus) dwelleth all the fullness of the Godhead bodily. (Colossians 2:9).

Know ye not your own selves, how that Jesus Christ is in you, except ye be reprobates. (2 Corinthians 13:5)

So if Christ is, and has the fullness of God; and if he indwells us, then to speak of having 200% or more of Him is patently ridiculous, and more to the point, un-Biblical. It is in effect, a sort of 'one-upmanship', or desiring to be 'the greatest'. Let us remember that Jesus censured those who sought to be the greatest.

Problems begin when the anointing presence of the Holy Spirit is incorrectly attributed to the person through whom He is working.

This lies at the heart of the erroneous teaching that some people have a 'special anointing'. This teaching creates a two, or sometimes three-tier level of Christians, and goes against all reasonable exegesis of the relevant passages of Scripture.

Does the Holy Spirit manifest His presence in a more tangible and powerful way through certain individuals? Yes He does. There are many examples, past and present, where this is so.

Does that set this person apart from, or over and above, other believers? No! It is the Person and Presence of the Holy Spirit that is to be honored, and not the person He is using.

As in all the ages that have gone before, today's church is awash with strange doctrines and strange ideas, and our only defense is to check them against Scripture.

These (the Bereans) were more noble than those in Thessalonica, in that they received the word with all readiness of mind, and searched the Scriptures daily, whether those things were so. (Acts 17: 11)

According to the New Testament, and evidence drawn from the post Pentecost church, the truth about anointing is that Jesus Christ *is* the anointing.

By the Holy Spirit's indwelling presence all born-again believers have that anointing. Every born-again believer has the authority that accompanies it, and should exercise their God given authority against the works of the devil, not against each other.

The erroneous teachings regarding the anointing are compounded when linked to the man-made tradition of ordination. Ordination, as it is currently practiced, negates the equality of the members of the body, having Christ as its head. The Protestant office of pastor clearly descends from the Roman Catholic office of priest, which in turn is derived from pagan cultic practices.

The desire of the heart of most pastors is for their flock to be an effective witness of the gospel to the world. Paradoxically, the 'office' that they hold is one of the greatest hindrances to the achievement of their hearts desire.

God's plan is that none should perish (2 Peter 3:9). The effectiveness of the church to carry out His plan is hindered and weakened by the elevation of some Christians to a false position of superiority. The elevation of the 'office' of Priest and Pastor above the other members of the ekklesia (every one of whom is a royal priest) is clearly at odds with the original blueprint for the church.

There are many other examples where man-made stones are out of alignment with Jesus Christ, the cornerstone. Clearly the origins of most aspects of contemporary church practice are rooted in secular pagan practices.

There seems to be two alternative courses of action; the first is to discard everything in contemporary church practice that is not part of the first century model; a model that was suited to that time and place, but may not necessarily fit neatly into the twenty-first century.

The second, and possibly the more appropriate course, is to develop our understanding of where the current practices spring from and which of them are central to being an authentic follower of Jesus Christ.

Then, being freed from man-made traditions and impositions, we can make appropriate choices and decisions that suit our own particular time and circumstances.

If this book has helped you in being able to do that, then it has achieved its purpose.

CHAPTER FIFTEEN
Onward Christian Soldiers

From the earliest evidence of civilization some 8,000 years ago, to the complex and varied cultures in the modern world, there are many strands in the history of the human race. In this book we have followed one, the on-going revelation and purpose of God the Creator, toward mankind.

One of the other major strands is the pursuit of knowledge. While untold millions die of starvation and lack of clean water, the search for knowledge is relentless. It drives mankind to spend millions of dollars to send probes to the furthest depths of the universe.

Even more millions are spent on trying to find the make up of matter and what it is that holds this universe together. There seem to be no limitations on where mankind will go in the endless search for knowledge, even to the point of discovering the source of, and even to artificially create, life itself.

Yet the answer is there for us if we would but look in the right direction. From the moment that Abram heard God, and responded to the call to move from Ur to Canaan, right up to the present day, God's redemptive plan of salvation has been at work.

"The idea that God entered the world in human form, was crucified and rose from the dead seems incredible to many. Yet the world is a far different place than it would be if there had not been millions who believed and proclaimed this message. How many hospitals, how many institutions of higher education have come into being because of the driving force of those who

went forth in the name of the one whom they believed to be God Incarnate! The impact that Christianity had on the first century world and the subsequent development of history is directly related to the revolutionary ideas that it presented about who Jesus Christ is and what the meaning of life is".xxxii

The ekklesia of God, the church, was the instrument by which he intended to communicate his purpose and the free offer of eternal life. The original blueprint for the church was that it should be constructed in alignment with Jesus Christ the cornerstone.

The plan was based on relational groups rather than hierarchical organizations.

The relationship of the individual with God the Father was made possible by the once and for all time sacrifice of Jesus Christ, the Son (Hebrews 9:12).

The assurance of that relationship came by Christ coming to abide with the believer. (Galatians 2:20 and Colossians1:27)

The ability to walk out that relationship with God, and with other believers in the body of Christ, was made possible by the effective presence of the Holy Spirit within each believer. (Romans 8:9-11)

As we have seen, there have been many diversions and additions that would seem to frustrate God's purpose. Those we have looked at in the preceding chapters are but a few of the myriad of events, doctrines and theological missteps that have sought to misalign the 'building' from the cornerstone.

In this day and age, when the secularization of our culture seems to be gaining pace and the Christian faith is under increasing attack, it is vital that we pursue authentic truth, the truth that sets us (and the world) free.

"That is to say, it is on the one side confronted by a society that no longer claims to be Christian in any sense, and on the other side it is subjected to challenge and even persecution. In these conditions the authenticity of faith, attentive listening to God's Word, the informing of every day life by the Christian spirit and boldness of witness becomes once more the true face of revelation.[xxxiii]

Ordinary Christians should be able to step out with bold confidence and exercise their faith in who they truly are in Christ Jesus.

In pointing out the pagan influences that have detracted from their ability to do this, I am not suggesting that war be waged on 'Christian' institutions and organizations. For better or worse they are part of contemporary Christianity, and God uses them and the people who work within them.

At the end of the day, all these things will pass away and the only stone left standing will be Jesus Christ, ***the*** cornerstone.

Just like diners in a restaurant we can elect to go for the surroundings, the ambience, the starched linen, the silverware, and the efficient service and put up with the poor fare, or we can seek true sustenance and make that our reason for dining.

Jesus says that he is the Way, the Truth and the Life (John 14:6) and that the Truth will set us free (John 8:32). The information presented in this book about the development of the church, and the various influences that have distorted its path, is aimed at helping you see the truth.

"Beware lest any man spoil you through philosophy and vain deceit, after the tradition of men, after the rudiments of the world, and not after Christ". (Colossians 2:8)

"Making the word of God of none effect through your traditions, which ye have delivered; and many such like things do ye," (Mark7:13)

Whatever you, the reader, decide to do, just remember that ultimately God will be triumphant.

"Again and again in the course of history it is in these conditions (challenge and persecution) *that we have seen the truth reappear unchanged, caught up by the revelation, caught up again, incarnated, carried not by heroes but by humble and devout people of all kinds who do not leave their names to posterity".xxxiv*

As one humble Christian to another, I hope that this book has helped you in your own walk of faith, and that you will be encouraged to step out with boldness as an ambassador for Christ, having no doubts as to your ability to do all things through Christ who dwells within you.

####

APPENDICES

APPENDIX ONE
Basilicas, Church Buildings and Pagan Practices.

- Both faced East toward the rising sun.
- The magistrate's chair, the *cathedra*, became the Bishop's chair.
- The *ambo* from which speeches were made became the central speaker's stand and named the Pulpit when on the left and the Lectern when on the right.
- The *Apse* was a special area at one end of the basilica and it became the area for the altar and bishop's chair.
- The rail that separated the important officials from the pulpit became the altar rail to separate the 'sacred' area from the public.
- The *nave* where the passive audience observed and listened to the proceedings became the nave where the non-clergy congregation sat.
- Later on an extension was added to form a cross. It is known as the *transept*.

Various pagan practices were also taken up.

- The *processional lights* are seen in the candles coming in with the clergy.
- The burning of *aromatic spices* became the burning of incense.
- The *special robes* that denoted the official's function and rank became the clergy robes styled on that of Roman officials.
- The *processional music* became choirs and praise and worship teams.

The Pagan roots of church buildings and contemporary 'Christian' practice is quite clear.

APPENDIX TWO
Typical Elements of The Contemporary Protestant Church Service.

- The greeting at the door with a handshake.
- Given a pre-determined order of service and shown to a seat.
- A greeting from the pulpit.
- A prayer or Scripture reading. Chapter and verse decided beforehand with a person appointed to read it.
- Hymns and songs. Led by a choir or music team.
- The 'spontaneous' songs are practiced mid-week to ensure a professional performance.
- The Announcements and the Offering. Prefaced by an Old Testament reference to tithing and sometimes accompanied by a song.
- The Sermon delivered from the platform usually by the same person each week.
- The Lord's Supper at varying intervals depending on the pre-determined practice.
- Prayers and more singing followed by a formal dismissal or casual 'God bless you'.
- An after the service coffee.

A Fixed Format Repeated Each Week With Little Or No Opportunity For Spontaneity.

APPENDIX THREE
The Lack of Biblical Basis For The Contemporary Sermon.

- It is a regular occurrence whereas in both the Old and New Testaments it is not.
- It is delivered by the same person, rather than many different prophets within the same period or a person led by the Holy Spirit.
- It is a monologue delivered to a passive audience rather than a conversational dialogue that encourages active participation.
- It has a specific structure rather than extemporaneously without rhetorical structure and led by the Holy Spirit.

Neither the Old nor the New Testaments support the Sermon as it is currently held in the contemporary church.

END NOTES

[i] .(Chandler, T. (1987), Four Thousand Years of Urban Growth: An Historical Census, Edwin Mellon Press, Lewiston, New York, NY)

[ii] (Angus Madison. The World Economy: A Millenial Perspective. Organization for Economic Cooperation and Development. 2001. pp 98,242)

[iii] (Everett Ferguson. Backgrounds of Early Christianity. Erdmans Grand Rapids Michigan 1987.p257)

[iv] (Everett Ferguson. Backgrounds of Early Christianity. Erdmans Grand Rapids Michigan 1987.p165)

[v] (Everett Ferguson. Backgrounds of Early Christianity. Erdmans Grand Rapids Michigan 1987.p29)

[vi] (Brad Young.Jesus The Jewish Theologian. Hendrickson Publishers Peabody MS p.xii).

[vii] (Brad Young.Jesus The Jewish Theologian. Hendrickson Publishers Peabody MS p.xii).

[viii] ." (Brad Young. Jesus The Jewish Theologian. Hendrickson Publishers Peabody MS p.xxiii).

[ix] (Dr. Jeffrey L Seif. The Evolution of a Revelotion. University Press of America. 1994.p.53).

[x] (Dr.Eddie L Hyatt. 2000 Years of Charismatic Christianity. Hyatt International ministries.1998.p.8)

[xi] (Everett Ferguson. Backgrounds of Early Christianity. Erdmans Grand Rapids Michigan 1987.p39).

[xii] (Jaques Ellul. The Subversion of Christianity. Grand Rapids Michigan. 1991.p124).

[xiii] Tony Lane. Harper's Concise Book of Christian Faith. Lion Publishing. 1984.p.70.

[xiv] Paul K Davis.100 Decisive Battles from Ancient Times to the Present. Oxford University Press. New York.2001

[xv] Jaques Ellul. The Subversion of Christianity. Eerdmans Grand Rapids Michigan.1991 p.102

[xvi] Dr.Eddie L Hyatt. 2000 Years of Charismatic Christianity. Hyatt International ministries.1998.p.30

[xvii] Millard J Erickson. Christian Theology Second Edition. Baker Books Grand Rapids Michigan 2007.p.1081

[xviii] Millard J Erickson. Christian Theology Second Edition. Baker Books Grand Rapids Michigan 2007.p.1084

[xix] Dr. A. Nyland. The Source With Extensive Notes on Greek Word Meaning. Smith and Stirling Publishing Parramatta Australia 2004.

[xx] Findley B Edge. A Quest For Vitality in Religion: A Theological Approach to Religious Education. Broadman Nashville 1963.p.22

xxi *Dr.Eddie L Hyatt. 2000 Years of Charismatic Christianity. Hyatt International Ministries.1998.p.2).*

xxii *Frank Viola, George Barna. Pagan Christianity. Tyndale. Carol Stream Illinoise 2002. p.41*

xxiii *Frank Viola, George Barna. Pagan Christianity. Tyndale. Carol Stream Illinoise 2002. p.192*

xxiv *Everett Ferguson. Backgrounds of Early Christianity. Eerdmans Grand Rapids Michigan 1987.p173*

xxv *Will Durant. Caesar and Christ. Simon & Schuster. New York 1950. p.618,619*

xxvi *James F White. Protestant Worship. John Knox Press Westminster 1989.p.41-41*

xxvii *Frank Viola, George Barna. Pagan Christianity. Tyndale. Carol Stream Illinoise 2002. p.41*

xxviii *Everett Ferguson. Backgrounds of Early Christianity. Eerdmans Grand Rapids Michigan 1987.p173*

xxix *Hans Lewy. John Chrysostom in Encyclopaedia Judaica. Keter Publishing House 1997. CD Rom Edition.*

xxx *Frank Viola, George Barna. Pagan Christianity. Tyndale. Carol Stream Illinoise 2002. p.102*

xxxi *Frank Viola, George Barna. Pagan Christianity. Tyndale. Carol Stream Illinoise 2002. p.127*

xxxii *Millard J Erickson. Christian Theology. Second Edition. Baker Books Grand Rapids Michigan 1991. p.1250*

xxxiii *Jaques Ellul. The Subversion of Christianity. Eerdmans Grand Rapids Michigan 1991. p.208*

xxxiv *Jaques Ellul. The Subversion of Christianity. Eerdmans Grand Rapids Michigan 1991. p.208.*

www.ingramcontent.com/pod-product-compliance
Lightning Source LLC
Chambersburg PA
CBHW030108070426
42448CB00036B/481